MODERN

EDUCATIONAL

DANCE

Revised Edition

By *Valerie Preston-Dunlop*

Plays Inc., *Publishers,* Boston, MA

© Macdonald & Evans Ltd 1980

1990 Edition published by Plays, Inc.

First published in Great Britain by Macdonald & Evans Ltd in 1963
as *Modern Educational Dance*
Second edition published in 1980 as *A Handbook for Dance in Education*
Reprinted by Longman Group UK Ltd 1986

Library of Congress Cataloging-in-Publication Data

Preston-Dunlop, Valerie Monthland.
    Modern educational dance

    New ed. of A handbook for modern educational dance. 1980
    Includes bibliographical references (p.) and index.
    1. Dancing—Study and teaching. 2. Movement education.
3. Movement, Psychology of. 4. Laban, Rudolf von, 1879-1958.
I. Preston-Dunlop, Valerie Monthland. Handbook for modern
educational dance. II. Title.
GV1589.P74   1990   792.8—dc20   90-36091 CIP
ISBN 0-8238-0292-2

Printed in the United States of America

Preface to the Second Edition

This book is intended for all those interested in dance, especially people concerned with teaching and studying dance. Those who have taught dance in primary, secondary, or tertiary education for some time will notice that in this edition there is a shift in the treatment of the material in the sixteen Themes. Dance is now regarded as a three-stranded subject, namely performing, making, and appreciating dance, and effective work in any one area is seen as dependent on the other two. Throughout the first edition, stress was laid on experiencing movement, on coming to know through doing. The goals were not distinguished into the three strands of today, but were whole-heartedly experiential. This approach has been clearly shown to have its strengths, and also its shortcomings, which are: the lack of evaluative possibility through the private nature of experience, the lack of link with dance as a theatre art, the concentration on personal development, and the minimal stress on the acquisition of skill and on coming to appreciate, and to know, dance works through both feeling and cognition.

In this second edition, I attempt to bridge the gap by putting beside the experiential aims and descriptions, which must continue, the more publicly evaluable aspects of art education. Each teacher will decide, according to his situation, how he intends to stress his work; on skills or creativity, on public or private event, on classic or romantic methods. In this book I make clear my position, which is that an amalgam of these two poles is possible and fruitful. It is done not by juxtaposing technique sessions with creativity sessions, but by coming to have intimate knowledge of the utter dependence of the one on the other if successful dance work is to be achieved in education.

A group of children or young people dancing now might be working in unison at a technical body task, in small groups on a movement problem-solving task, or in twos on making. They may be practising for a recital or for an examination, or be engrossed in a film. They may be able to talk about dynamics and space, about pliés and contractions, falls and thrusts, dimensions and body design, and be as at home in ballet, modern, folk and disco dancing. Fundamentally they will be concerned with an art form, performing it, making it, and appreciating it, and be coming to know the nature of aesthetic experience. They should be helped to awareness of the place of dance in the context of the other arts, to some knowledge of its place in history, and to know how dance movements are related to behavioural movements. Sensitivity to quality and in human contact is an aim, skill acquisition in mastering and confidence in the medium of movement is another, acquaintance with the creative process as an occasional climactic experience of making is a third, knowledge of and accuracy in spatial organisation is a fourth, and enjoyment of dance works is a fifth.

When the stress is on dance as an art, there is a danger that the dance becomes more important than the dancers who are learning through it. Personal development of each individual towards autonomy must be a teacher's primary aim, and it is my contention that the kind of learning which disciplined, creative art subjects provide is fundamentally important to this process. They provide a way of coming to know which takes account of the fact that feeling, of the affective kind and the sensory kind, provides an avenue to knowledge, and dance provides an avenue with especially strong haptic, logical, aesthetic, and social strands.

This book aims to supply a systematic approach to knowing through dancing and knowing about dancing, by providing themes which are progressive ways of looking at the three aspects of dance teaching, namely performing, making, and appreciating. In no way can this book take the place of a teacher, for there is only one way to start knowing dance and that is by dancing. There must be a period of experiencing under a sensitive and informed teacher to lay the foundation for successful skills, creativity, and criticism.

January 1980   V. P–D.

Acknowledgments
to the First Edition

I am deeply indebted to Rudolf Laban for the inspiration and help that he gave me during my training and the ten years between this and his death. That I could not have written this book without him is so obvious that I need not stress the point. My thanks are also due to Miss Lisa Ullmann, Director of the Laban Art of Movement Centre, to whom I owe the major part of my training and who gave me valuable assistance with the text; to Margaret Rosewarne, Principal Lecturer at Bedford College of Physical Education, for her collaboration in compiling the scheme of work for the secondary age; to Miss Edith Alexander, late Principal of Dartford College of Physical Education, who for eight years supported my work in her college; to my sister Elizabeth Fisher for advice on musical matters; and to my husband who has not only put up with this book but, by challenging every word of it, has helped me to say what I mean. There are many people who have helped me by typing, reading, discussing and encouraging and I am grateful to them all.
(January 1963)

Acknowledgments
to the Second Edition

I acknowledge with gratitude the guidance of Mary Killick and Jacob Zelinger, who turned my thoughts to the nature of teaching and learning during Diploma of Education and M.A. studies, and also the generous support of Dr. Marion North. I cannot ignore my family, increased by two since the first edition; the younger foregoes cuddles, the elder foregoes help with prep, while I write. My husband is still challenging, and without his encouragement and actual help, his tolerance of my impossible hours, I would have to give in. Thank you all.

Contents

Introduction

The influence of Rudolf Laban on dance is profound. His iconoclastic career produced dozens of students who, all over the world, have made fundamental contributions to the evolution of the dance, in both theatre and school. 1979 saw his centenary, and it is not therefore surprising that the phenomenal ideas he put forward are now being used in guises other than those he first gave them. Enormous changes have taken place in dance; much more now is understood which illuminates Laban's attempts to provide a new rationale and meaning for dance. The work done now may no longer be recognisable in style as his work yet it fundamentally rests on the logic of his suggestions.

This book is founded on the Sixteen Basic Movement Themes put forward by him in 1948 in his *Modern Educational Dance*. They posited what was a revolutionary method at that time, together with systematic treatment of dance material. Methods have changed, goals have changed, so has dance and so have the expectations and abilities of young people, but the material of movement has remained. In the second edition of this book I have therefore taken the movement material and removed it from the strongly creative methods associated with Modern Educational Dance. In their place are methods more in line with the notions of aesthetic education today. The narrow concept of modern educational dance has been replaced by the wider-based concept of dance-as-art. I have been influenced by the discussions of learned men and women, by Hirst's examination of forms of knowledge, by Reid's stress on feeling as essential to knowing, by Polanyi's broadening of the ways of knowing, by Perry's emphasis on skill in making, by Ghiselin on creativity by Bruner and Piaget on the growth of competency.

Additionally, descriptions of the movement material have been updated to take into account recent work on dynamics and effort and spatial organisation. Here Lamb's action profiling and North's personality assessment, Bartenieff's fundamentals, combined with perception studies such as Gibson's are all influential. My own work in ergonomics with Professor Corlett and Professor Gedye added a dimension to my understanding of effort in work, and thence in dance. My investigations into choreutic notions were influenced by Rogers's sculptural analysis, Arnheim's art and visual perception enlightment, and by searching for choreutic forms in choreographies by Graham, Limón, Bruce, Macmillan, Cunningham, Nikolais, Humphrey, Ashton, Balanchine, *et al.*

Because of these basic changes, some of the original titles of the Themes seemed to be inaccurate, misleading or too narrow in concept. I have therefore changed them. The word "awareness" in the titles of Themes I–IV, VII, and IX was ambiguous. In all these Themes the work includes perceptual sensitising, skill development, making and the appreciating of dances. I cannot see that awareness goes far enough.

The word "effort" is used with the word "dynamics". While effort is an accurate word, it is unfortunately not at all dance-like. Dynamics is used in other art fields. I therefore use both.

Technique is mentioned many times and I intentionally do not recommend any of the current dance "techniques" for the development of skills in young bodies. I take the stand that neither Graham, Cunningham, Leeder nor ballet, the four with which I have some acquaintance, are suitable. That does not mean that student dance teachers should not learn them; on the contrary they must. But throughout I posit that technique should be acquired by the young in connection with making and appreciating, and not in isolation. It also does not mean that extra-curricular dance technique classes should not be available for those who want it; they should. Professor Wall's assertion that too much dance technique does to young bodies what Japanese foot-binding did to the feet of their young is salutary. In Cohen, Ellfeldt, and Nadel & Nadel, choreographers bemoan the dancer who is all technique with no artistry. Let us beware of the trap, and try to solve the problem.

How to organise dance to be enjoyed by both performer and audience is included. Here Lange's theory of art and Reid's creative embodiment theory of aesthetic appreciation, together with Osborne and Hospers, have been influential.

The link of dance with non-verbal communication is included, and the relationship of both to linguistic studies and body image theories. Lyons, Hinde, Argyle, Birdwhistell, Schilder all enlightened.

The parts of Theme XI (spatial orientation) dealing with choreutics have been removed to an Appendix II. This is such a vast subject, and one which I now see fundamentally in another light, that it cannot be included within the Themes. Similarly the more advanced effort work is in an Appendix I separately.

Because the whole area of schemes of work for primary, secondary, and tertiary education, and methods of teaching, is a colossal study, not possible to condense into one written chapter, I have omitted it altogether. Instead I have attempted to insert into the Themes sufficient variety of method and width of difficulty and progression that teachers will be able to use the Themes in whatever work situation they have.

For readers new to the sixteen Themes, the following condensation may be helpful.

Theme I: the possible ways of using the body in movement are introduced in connection with the sensitising of the kinesthetic perceptual system and the start of body skill acquisition.

Theme II: the concentration is here on the two elements of rhythm, weight and time, and the introduction of the concept of quality.

Theme III: the kinesphere and the general space is introduced, including the basic spatial actions.

Theme IV: the different aspects of the flow of movement is explained and used to form and appreciate movement phrases.

Theme V: dancing with someone and for someone is studied.

Theme VI: the cardinal combinations of movement qualities which form the eight basic effort actions are introduced as dynamic starting points.

Theme IX: the ability to make movement patterns in the kinesphere and with the body is developed and used in dance.

Theme X: dynamic rhythms and effort transitions are presented further.

Theme XI: spatial organisation is explained and used in forming and seeing form.

Theme XII: the relationship between the form and content of movement is studied.

Theme XIII: the bodily skill required for elevation is developed and the feeling of it in dance is experienced.

Theme XIV: group experiences and composition are begun.

Theme XV: form is given to the content of work in Theme XIV.

Theme XVI: the content of work in the previous Themes is here integrated and compositional topics necessary for choreography are studied.

It will be seen from the summary, and can be further understood from the full text of each Theme, that there is a progression of work from Theme I to Theme XVI. The relationship of one Theme to another is described in Chapter 17.

Within the text will be found symbols with which the essentials of the movement being described can be written down. These consist of the Effort Graph, and the body and direction signs from Laban's Kinetography, the method of writing movement in notation form which he invented. The effort graph consists of a diagonal stroke to which vertical and horizontal strokes are attached to represent the four motion factors Weight, Space, Time, and Flow. This is explained in Themes II, IV, and VII.

The kinetographic direction signs are used mainly in Theme XI and touched upon in Theme III. Various methods are used to identify the directions and teachers may use whichever they prefer. The following table lists the methods used in the text.

direction	"high"	is written	H or Ø
"	"deep"	"	D or ∎
"	"to the right"	"	R or ▷
"	"to the left"	"	L or ◁
"	"forwards"	"	F or ⬡
"	"backwards"	"	B or ⬡
"	"centre"	"	C or ⬡

direction	"diagonal high-right-forwards"	is written	HRF or Ø
"	"	deep-left-backwards"	"	DLB or ∎
"	"	high-left-forwards"	"	HLF or ⬡
"	"	deep-right-backwards"	"	DRB or ∎
"	"	high-left-backwards"	"	HLB or ⬡
"	"	deep-right-forwards"	"	DRF or ∎
"	"	high-right-backwards"	"	HRB or ⬡
"	"	deep-left-forwards"	"	DLF or ∎

direction	"high-right"	is written	HR or ▷
"	"right-backwards"	"	RB or ◁
"	"backwards-deep"	"	BD or ∎
"	"deep-right"	"	DR or ▷
"	"right-forwards"	"	RF or ◁
"	"forwards-deep"	"	FD or ∎
"	"deep-left"	"	DL or ◀
"	"left-forwards"	"	LF or ⬡
"	"forwards-high"	"	FH or ⬡
"	"high-left"	"	HL or ◁
"	"left-backwards"	"	LB or ⬡
"	"backwards-high"	"	BH or ⬡

These symbols are included because the description of movement in words is difficult and clumsy. This is not so apparent in the early Themes as the movement principles involved are of a simple nature, but as the Themes become more advanced the symbols obviate lengthy descriptions.

The symbols for the parts of the body which are illustrated on page 5 are not used again and may seem superfluous but are included so that the reader may see that the three aspects of movement, the part of the body moved, the direction in space of it, and the quality with which it is done, can all be notated. No attempt is made to show how the three sets of symbols are combined to make a comprehensive method of notation as this is a complete study in itself. (*See* Laban R. 1975; Hutchinson A. 1970; Preston-Dunlop V. 1969; Knust A. 1979.) Any of the symbols may be used as visual aids during the teaching of movement and dance; children find them easy to pick up and enjoy writing, in simple terms, their own inventions.

CHAPTER 1

Theme I: Introduction to the Body

The kinesthetic sense (Gibson J. J. 1966) is the dancer's source of information. This Theme looks at it from the point of view of the body's parts, and their most elementary kinetic functions. It aims to draw attention to the fact that knowledge and feeling of the body's parts need to be built up. The message network of muscle, bone, nerve, brain, judgment (and its reverse) needs to become efficient, reliable, and increasingly sensitive. Here the elements concerned with body, only, are discussed, under the six sub-headings.

The kinesthetic sense relays muscular, articular, cutaneous, vestibular, visual, and auditory cues to the brain. These messages inform the mover of facts about the muscle tension, balance, and relevant sights and sounds, which ne learns to interpret in terms of movements made and positions achieved.

Bending, stretching and twisting are the basic mechanical constituents of movement. Each part of this Theme is based on particular manners of moving which co-ordinate the bend, stretch and twist in different ways. Each is also designed to encourage kinesthetic knowledge of the relationships between the different parts of the body so that they can work together and assist one another in producing co-ordinated movement. The job of the kinesthetic sense, therefore, is to relay what is happening in and to the body, and which parts are or are not acting as they should, and in what manner.

1. THE BODY IN MOTION AND STILLNESS

It is unusual in modern adult life to use or conceive of the body as a whole, as so many activities demand the specialised use of small parts of the body. The child, however, has a feeling for whole body movement and herein lies his advantage for it is essential in dance. Movements such as opening, closing, twisting, turning, running, skipping, walking, crouching, rising, falling or leaping can be used and children encouraged to use and to sense the whole body in each, the focus being on the contribution which each part of the body makes to the action. The spine and head are the parts of the body most likely to be unco-ordinated and unsensing, and a teacher can remind the class of these and any other parts which he sees are not yet alert.

With beginners activity usually tails off after an action is done, there being no clear moment of completion, but the latter should be encouraged by giving importance to the completion by staying still for a moment after it. Stillness is by no means analogous to "at rest" or "relaxed" nor is it a passive state. The stillness should be a clear position which is as full of kinesthetic feeling as the action which preceded it. Muscular tension is easy to feel in held positions, and laying stress on this aids the education of the kinesthetic sense. The messages via the kinesthetic network are here not about dynamics, or shape, or direction, or speed, or other people, or placement in a room but about the dancer's own body. The concept "my moving body" is being built up. Obviously an infant and a teenager will have quite different concept possibilities and problems, but in each case the subject matter "my body" is the same. The teaching situation framework, however, is unique to each teacher and each class and each group of individuals. It may consist of learning to achieve sequences of actions, or of exploring the possibilities of twisting, or of looking at a video of more experienced dancers' "falling and recovery" sequences.

2. SYMMETRIC AND ASYMMETRIC USE OF THE BODY

The body has an ideational division, by way of the spine,

into two halves, the right and the left. Asymmetric movement, where one side is more active than the other, is felt as a sensation of inequality. This is countered by symmetric movement which has equal stress by both sides and is experienced as a state of equalness. Symmetric notions are usually associated with body design (Weyl H. 1952); the patterns and positions made by one side are taken as mirrored on the other side; complete similarity of design is meant. However, symmetry may also be taken as equality of activity, equality of tension, equality of intention. In each of these cases, equality of design is partial, and may even be absent.

Symmetry in time means that a phrase is repeated with lateral inversion, i.e. symmetrically. What was done with the right is now done with the left; right turns become left turns.

The kinesthetic sensing requirement is self-evident (basically the concept "I have two sides" is being built up) and the alertness and control needed to use this concept in dancing, and in composition, skilfully, is gradually acquired.

Most dance sequences contain elements of symmetry. Youngsters' attention can be brought to these occurrences in their own dancing. Younger children enjoy working on a simple task like "do the same on the other side", while older children may well be absorbed in some longer-term activity and find symmetric ideas helpful in that context, and boring out of context. When making a dance with symmetric repeats, craftsman's decisions have to be made to achieve satisfactory transitions. Seeing how another person uses symmetry and asymmetry in a composition is interesting and engages the critical faculties.

3. EMPHASIS ON PARTS OF THE BODY

Movement begins to be articulated when certain parts of the body take an independent role, as when certain sections of an orchestra are heard independently of the others. This may be apparent simply as a sensing exercise, when special attention is paid to a particular part. It may be apparent in focusing attention on one part of another's moving body.

The role of the legs in stepping, locomotion, falling and

elevation is crucial. Their task is to carry the upper part of
the body while making co-ordinated changes themselves.
Muscular clusters tensing and relaxing can be felt as the
motor system learns to control the legs' actions. The arms
move through the space, twisting, gathering, reaching,
spiralling; they must co-ordinate with the supporting legs
somehow.

All movements of the body are dependent on sensing,
suppleness, strength and control of the trunk. The spine has
a range and an ability to pull out, arch, bend and twist. The
muscular wall of the front of the body can be contracted,
be flabby, taut, or stretched. The manner in which the arms
are attached to the body at the shoulder area can be attended
to, and the range become known. The manner in which the
legs are attached, the strong muscle clusters in the seat and
groin, which control their twisting ability and their lifting
ability, can be felt. The way the head is attached to the
body and the feel of the neck and its range can become
known. Teachers cause the ways of coming to know to suit
all manner of children and their needs. As examples of what
might be done, the flabbiness and tautness of the abdominal
wall can be felt for the fun of it; technical exercises aimed
at development of the spine can be practised; arms and legs
can be used as solo "voices" in a conversation for body
parts; the way reaching arms take the trunk along too can be
explored, the contextual significance of an isolated head turn
can be discussed.

4. ATTENTION TO SPECIFIC PARTS OF THE BODY

The natural progression of articulation from having a whole
area of the body predominant is to take more specific parts.
Movements of the body led by the arms are clarified when
attention is paid to the shoulder, elbow, wrist, hand, or
surfaces of the arm. All can be alert, all can lead all can be
sensed. The hand particularly has many possibilities of
further differentiation in the palm, finger tips, back of the
hand and little finger side.

The legs have similar possibilities. The hip, knee, heel, and
foot are all suitable for leading the leg into gestures and steps.

The feet and ankles require special attention. They are fundamental to dancers, both functionally and aesthetically. The
dancer's relationship with the floor is through the feet more
often than not, and how this is varied and controlled must
become known gradually. Sensitive and reliable kinesthetic
messages from the feet and ankles are priorities.

The chest and pelvic girdle and the waist together comprise
the trunk. The surfaces of the parts of the trunk, the skeletal
parts of it, the muscular parts of it, need to become known in
movement and in stillness, in isolation and in co-ordination.
The muscles between the ribs may be moved and sensed. The
vulnerability of the waist may be exposed by over-zealous
arching and inadequate control. The shoulders, the chest, the
pelvis may twist independently of one another. The breast

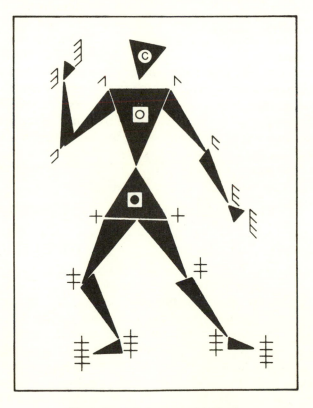

Fig. 1. *Symbols for parts of the body.*

bone may lead a rising movement of the whole body; the lifting and tensing of the pelvis area may lead a recovery from lying.

All manner of sequences can be danced where particular parts of the body lead an action. "Leading with" is an especial dance activity of the body which is worthy of special attention. The teacher can create short dances in which the leading possibilities of particular areas of the body are studied; for example:

> (a) a fairly slow dance where the joints and surfaces of the arms lead the movements, until an end position which physically requires change of leadership is achieved;
> (b) a quicker dance where jumps are used with parts of the legs leading the gestures;
> (c) a sequence where surfaces of the trunk focus on parts of the room.

The teacher can also leave the children free to choose their actions, although giving the part of the body which is to lead, or the shape can be given and the leading part of the body be left to the child's choice. Two people can work together, the one showing that he has seen what part the other is leading with by making a movement with the same part leading. All manner of situations can be given by the teacher to suit the needs of the group being taught.

5. WEIGHT TRANSFERENCE AND GESTURE

The first sensing to be done under this heading is of the difference between bearing weight and not bearing weight. The concepts "my body is supported", "my body part is free" and "these body parts are supporting me" are fundamental. Following this comes the variety of ways in which the supporting might be achieved. Because of the upright carriage of the human race, the legs are the natural instruments of transference. The feet which are the usual weight bearers can be made aware of the many shades of expression of which they are capable. The toes, the ball of the foot and the heel can become sensitive to the floor and to the various rhythms of stepping, such as rolling the weight from the toe to the heel, from the heel to the toe. Varieties of kneeling and sitting can be the starting or culminating positions of movement phrases or intermediate stages. The body adjusts itself with every new support and finds a balance by gestures of the free limbs.

Sitting positions, lying positions, kneeling positions abound, as do ways of going from one to the other skilfully, aesthetically, boldly, swiftly. Here is the meat for hours of play and years of technique training, and every opportunity for kinesthetic sensing.

Although the arms are the natural limbs of gesture, they are required to bear weight in dance. Handstands, cartwheels and their varieties need a colossal kinesthetic adjustment in terms of sensing, practice and training. Shared weight bearing between hands, shoulders, back of head, knee, top of foot, lower arm, heel, diagonal chest surface, buttock are all possible, and need to become known.

The ways in which a teacher uses this Theme appropriately will provide skill, varied vocabulary, insight into possibilities, adventure, joy of achievement, the fun of trials and errors, and admiration for the skill of others.

6. RELATIONSHIPS OF PARTS OF THE BODY

The Schuhplattler is an example of a dance in which parts of the body are in contact with one another; the hands clap one another and also slap the thigh and the foot and the lower leg. Primitive people beat out rhythms on their bodies; Mediterranean races snap their fingers together for percussive accompaniment to their dances. But contact need not be audible or tactile. Two parts of the body can be near each other, gently touch, interlink, surround one another. They can go away from, avoid, go round each other. Both can be equally active or one part can dominate.

Step patterns can be looked at from this point of view. The feet are constantly meeting and parting both in the air and on the floor. They pass, beat, approach, touch.

The relationship of body parts is a co-ordination fundamental. Memory of positions and then of movements is helped when they are looked at in terms of relationship changes. Visual perception of a movement is not always, indeed often not fully possible. The kinesthetic sense has to relay the relationship of parts, surfaces, limbs, joints in order to provide the data for invention and control.

The teacher can create sequences for the class to dance which involve the relationship of parts of the body or can stimulate exploration and improvisation of these themes. He may himself demonstrate examples for central appraisal, perform several as examples of comedy, suggest watching T.V. dance from this point of view or aid in a search for relationships expressive of one child's ideas for a dance on the Nativity theme.

CHAPTER 2

Theme II: Introduction to Weight and Time

This Theme is the first of several dealing with the dynamics and rhythm of movement.

Dynamic and rhythmic changes are registered by the dancer through his kinesthetic sense, particularly through messages from the muscles and skin (Gibson J. J. 1966). The feelings sensed occur as complex changes. The changes are not discrete but continuous; they occur all over the body and are interwoven and difficult to discern so that all that can be attempted initially is to teach the dancer to notice certain major differences occuring at important moments in the movement.

Dynamic changes operate at two levels:

(a) in order to achieve technically and mechanically the movements in question;

(b) in order to colour those movements with dynamics other than those they require mechanically or technically.

For example, a jump requires energy changes which are muscular tension changes, acceleration and deceleration, in order to achieve take-off, height and aerial actions, and control of landing. However, the jump may be used in the context of a joyful vivacious solo, or a tense struggling duo, in an elegant or in a comic style. Obviously dynamic qualities over and above those required for technical achievement will be employed to help produce these effects. The two levels of dynamic have to be coped with by the teacher and the dancer, in that the skill of the technique is being learnt at one level while the qualitative expression is being found out at the second level.

The kinesthetic reception of dynamic changes depends on sensitising the body to changes of force and changes of speed, the technical terms being *weight and time changes*.

1. WEIGHT QUALITIES

In order to build up a concept of the weight factor in movement, several strands of information have to come together. The first strand is the *pull of gravity*. Unless force is exerted in a vertically upward direction equal to the downward pull of gravity, the body will fall. When upward exertion weakens, a feeling of weakness and heaviness is experienced.

The second strand is force exerted in action, *kinetic force*. The energy is used to move the body into space. It could be thought of as the energy needed to move the body.

The third strand is *static force;* it is exerted when a position is held in a state of active muscular tension. The force is not moving the body, but contained within the body. It feels as if internal resistance is being added to the movement.

Another strand is the *external resistance* provided by things and people. A partner, a piece of apparatus, a prop, furniture, can partially support the body, and can also resist being moved. This support and resistance is sensed as a dynamic condition.

There are then four strands:

(a) the pull of gravity to be overcome;
(b) kinetic force to move the body in space;
(c) static force within the body;
(d) external resistance to be overcome.

There are two ways in which each of these four strands can be dealt with dynamically, and these two ways are called *strongly* or *lightly*.

(a) heaviness can be countered lightly or strongly;
(b) body parts can be moved lightly or strongly;
(c) internal resistance can be given lightly or strongly;
(d) external resistance can be overcome lightly or strongly.

What do "lightly" and "strongly" mean in these connections? Basically they can be seen as a positive minimum-maximum continuum.

(a) *Light* anti-gravity exertion is the force upward, just sufficient to hold the skeletal structure poised and un-slumped. It is a very important dynamic tension for dancers. It is their basic condition which provides them with the kind of poise and carriage which sets dancing apart from most other moving.

(b) *Light* kinetic force is light anti-gravity exertion while moving the body or body part in any direction. The actual amount of force used will depend on the size of body part and leverage, but in all cases it is just sufficient to keep that sensation of light poised moving.

(c) *Light* static force is minimal bracing involving minimal tension and counter-tension.

(d) *Light* interaction with resistance from outside is again a minimum force, a light touch, a gentle push, a soft yield. The minimal force is produced in the opposite direction to the resistance.

Note: these minimal forces may occur independently or simultaneously or sequentially.

(a) *Strong* anti-gravity exertion occurs in the upward direction such that the skeletal frame is pulled further apart than in poised lightness. There is only one exertion equal to and opposite to the pull of gravity, and that is called "light".

(b) *Strong* kinetic force is produced when the body or body parts are moved forcefully. The anti-gravity upward exertion may be present, or may be absent, in which case a certain heaviness or feeling of momentum will be present. The speed of the movement radically alters the sensation and the behaviour. A strong slow movement must have static force, or external resistance to be called "strong", but a speedy, large movement may feel strong by reason of the need to overcome inertia.

(c) *Strong* static force occurs when there are internal counter-tensions producing a firm, braced condition. This strong static tension may be used in positions, or can accompany strong kinetic force as an addition. The tension may be in any direction, and is experienced as an internal resistance.

(d) *Strong* interaction with resistance from outside is without internal counter-tension; the energy is directed against a resistance. An anti-gravity component may or may not be present, with the accompanying sensations of poised power or relaxed power being felt.

Note: these four forces occur independently or simultaneously or sequentially.

So, it will be seen that the matter of strong and light force is a continuously exciting interchange of these four ways of moving.

Strength and lightness may be produced throughout a movement, in which case the whole movement will be done "strongly" or "lightly", be analysed as such, and sensed as such. However, many dance movements are not quite so simple, and the strength or lightness do not last throughout. But *moments* during the movement may especially be strongly or lightly achieved, as perhaps in a loud clap or in a skip: the moment is analysed as strong or light and sensed as a peak in the constantly changing situation.

To some of the four types of strength (anti-gravity, kinetic, static, or against resistance) words other than "strong" may be equally applicable. Strong static force can just as well be described by the word "firm", while for the kinetic force of a strong leap the word "vigorous" might serve. Light static tension may be described as "slight" tension, and light resistance could be described as "weak", a light touch as "delicate".

There will also be movements and moments in movement which are clearly neither strong nor light nor heavy; these things are crowded out of the perception because other qualities or considerations are more imposing. There is no reason to believe that it is helpful to attempt to analyse or discern the weight characteristic of every part of every movement.

The kinesthetic sense has a great deal of work to do in order to aid understanding and sensitive feeling of strong and light and heavy dynamics. So the teacher is going to provide opportunities for discerning, within the body, and, of seeing in someone else's body, these qualities. To ask for "a strong movement" is perhaps not very helpful, for the likelihood is that a very un-dance-like movement will result, most likely with clenched fists, and possibly with stamping feet.

No, dynamics can only materialise in the body, and the active body at that. Therefore, the teacher will want to go back to Theme I and use this vocabulary in which the dynamic changes can be felt. After all, dynamics is best seen as an adverb qualifying a "doing" verb.

So we have, as examples, opening lightly, twisting strongly, rising from a strong start, falling heavily, skipping lightly and heavily, stamping strongly, stamping heavily, being still lightly, coming to rest lightly, ending with a strong held position. Of course, a variety of words may be used.

Transferring weight, leading with body parts, relating body parts, can all be seen to be full of dynamic potential.

Alternatively, a much more advanced group may turn to this simple Theme II for basic analysis of some new material, possibly an ethnic dance being learnt, or rhythmic problems in a complicated accompaniment, or basic preparatory work for lifts in a duo, or just to realise that strength and lightness in another person is difficult, and on film is very difficult, to see.

2. TIME QUALITIES

Basically, a movement can take a long time to do or a short time. This is the *duration* of the movement. The distance covered in the duration determines the *speed* of the movement. Increases and decreases from one speed to another are common.

The three time facts are:

(a) that duration is on a continuum from very short to very long;

(b) that speed is on a continuum from very fast to very slow;

(c) that speed is not constant in movement, but changes: providing accelerating and decelerating moments during the movement.

Knowledge (Hirst P. H. 1972; Polanyi M. 1969) of the speed, the duration and the acceleration of the movement may be of an intellectual sort, and this has to be translated into a kinesthetic sort before it is useful to dancers. It has to be felt. The kinesthetic sense has to perceive the fast movement and the slow movement, and the fact of this fastness and slowness has to permeate the whole body so that the whole is sensed as a qualitative way of experiencing time in movement.

There are two ways in which the three strands are most commonly perceived dynamically. The resulting qualities are called *suddenness* and *sustainment.*

(a) Sudden quality is discerned in fast movement of short duration.

(b) Sudden quality is discerned in acceleration of short duration.

(c) Sustained quality is discerned in slow movement of longer duration.

(d) Sustained quality is discerned in deceleration of longer duration.

But other combinations, which are less obvious, are also discernible:

(e) Fast movement of long duration.

(f) Acceleration of long duration.

Both these presuppose that the movement is of a kind capable of continuing, such as travelling, turning, endless gesturing, vibrating.

(g) Short slow movement.

(h) Short deceleration.

These two are so small and brief that they are not easily discernible except as transitions.

Sudden moments in movement are perceived by the kinesthetic sense; words describing this sensing might be "urgent", "sharp", "staccato", "excited", "instantaneous", "hastening".

Sustained moments in movement are perceived by the kinesthetic sense; words describing the sensing might be "slow", "smooth", "legato", "prolonged", "lingering".

There will also be movements and moments in movement which are clearly neither sudden nor sustained. Other qualities are more significant in them. It is pointless to try to discern the time qualities in these cases.

All the actions in Theme I may be seen to contain time changes, and can become more interesting to do when attention is paid to the time changes. Skill in doing and in discerning these qualities, and visually perceiving them in others, builds up movement knowledge and competence. It is also great fun, sometimes exhilarating, sometimes calming.

3. WEIGHT-TIME QUALITIES

There will be moments in dancing when time qualities dominate, other moments when weight qualities dominate, and still others when both seem important.

These might occur as follows.

(a) *Strong-sustained* moments can be described as "concentrated", "powerful", "persevering". When this quality is in the whole body, the sensation is one of general firmness with static tension. It may well occur only in part of the body, for instance in the legs, perhaps in technical training, while the rest of the body feels light.

(b) *Light-sudden* moments can be described as "bright", "brisk", "crisp". When this quality is in the whole body, all manner of jumping, darting, prancing actions can be seen. It may also occur only in neat footwork, while the arms and trunk remain smooth, or in a staccato head turn, a fluttering hand, a sharp intake of breath.

(c) *Strong-sudden* moments can be described as "energetic", "vigorous", "athletic". The confined energy bursts out into vigorous action. The limbs beat their way through the air, stamping, whipping round, jumping. The quality may also be seen as a percussive slap, an aggressive shoulder twist, a central contraction.

(d) *Light-sustained* moments can be described as "peaceful", "soothing", "quiet", "unruffled". Smooth changes of position, delicate gestures, unhurried poise, sensitive contact, epitomise moments in this quality.

The qualities described in *(a)* to *(d)* are all on the positive weight continuum. In addition there are two more on the negative weight continuum, but real control of time in a heavy state is difficult:

(e) *Heavy-sustained* moments may occur, perhaps in rolling, or in a slow crumple.

(f) *Heavy-sudden* moments may occur: in a sudden drop, a quick flinging movement.

These qualities do not remain the same over long periods, but come and go in rhythmic changes. Some dances may contain one predominantly, but it is helpful to realise that dynamic movement involves changing qualities in phrases.

Play and learning situations should be provided in a variety of ways, including imitation and partner work. Percussion is very useful as the changes can be heard on most instruments; and the gong and large cymbal will provide sustainment. The children can dance to percussion which is played by the teacher or can play for themselves as they dance.

The unwary teacher may fasten on to these time-weight changes, and "teach" them out of context to children, forgetting that in dance they occur in phrases and slip into and out of one another. The more advanced the dance, the more likely are these dynamic qualities to mix and merge in flowing movement. Beginners can be encouraged to discern the different qualities, to produce them, to observe them, to play with them, master them, practise them, in order then to dance with them in mixtures.

4. METRE

Metre provides a way of analysing duration. It is time divided into measurable units. When movement is performed to conform with these units it is called metrical movement and much dance is metrical, especially that which is accompanied by music. The short and long units of time are relative to one another and are called breves, semi-breves, minims, crotchets, quavers, etc., half notes, quarter notes, etc.

People enjoy moving in a metrical way and listening to the metre in music and translating what they hear into movement. For example, with young beginners, a teacher can help the feeling for metre by using a drum beat as the stimulus to action, as follows:

(a) *Even crotchets*, the children bringing this out in the feet, by clapping or by short movements of any part of their body. The speed of the crotchet should approximate to that of the heart beat.

(b) *Even quavers*, so that speedier motion is asked for.

(c) *Even minims*, so that slower motion is asked for.

(d) *Even semi-breves*, by which really sustained movements are stimulated.

The drum beat can be varied within these four possibilities and the children will learn to change their speeds with the sound. The children can then make the variations themselves while the drum beat stays the same, forming repeatable sequences which a partner could pick up. The phrases will be very simple to start with, for example two crotchets, two quavers and another crotchet repeated, and become longer and more varied as skill is acquired. Dotted time values can be introduced and the difference between duple and triple time. Movement done in triple time is more flowing than that in duple and this difference can be shown. The children can learn to recognise the time signature of their movement and to change from one into another skilfully.

A more advanced group might play with metric durations using arbitrary or chance lengths, say 7, 2, 4, 1, 11, 3, 5. These lengths would have repetitions: 7, 7, 2, 2, 2, 4, 1, 1, 1, 11, 11, 3, 5, 3, 5.

They may interest themselves in these durations with actions, with stillness, with vibration, or unaccented movement. Or, perhaps they study how a choreographer has matched a movement to that of the accompaniment or has gone against it.

It is a fact that a very few people have great difficulty in conforming to a metre. They appear not to be able to translate a sound impression into a kinesthetic impression. They have their own rate of moving which they can not hasten or slow down. These few are arhythmic. A teacher can help such a dancer to cope with his problem, but in some cases it cannot be overcome.

5. RHYTHM

There are two kinds of rhythm, metric and non-metric. Without metre, something else has to take its place as an organiser of duration; sometimes the breath does, sometimes chance, sometimes free choice and sometimes action.

Rhythmic movement in dance is what is achieved or seen when a dynamic response to time and force is used with an organisation of duration and the unity is phrased to provide an aesthetic whole. This Theme does not encompass all the possibilities, but the basic skills and frontiers are presented to be achieved and approached.

Tasks to be worked on include combinations of the following:

(a) Actions of the body with dynamic changes:
   (i) walks which are thumping, on tiptoe, bouncy, smooth and slidy, tense, slow and stately;
   (ii) jumps which are light, vigorous, sparkling, precise;
   (iii) extensions which are pushing, weak, which shoot out suddenly;
   (iv) twists which are firm, gentle, which whip around;
   (v) stillnesses which happen suddenly, which arrive almost unseen, which freeze, which crumble.
(b) Repetitions into phrases, three of some movement or four, and a pause, or three and a transition onto the other side of the body.
(c) Phrase-making with different dynamics, entirely with walks or selected qualities, entirely with imaginative movements which are all about quality only: toughness, gallumphingness, squidginess.
(d) With regular metres, walking in 3/4, 4/4, in iambic, in dactylic, jumping in 6/8 and 2/4; holding still for a whole bar, moving for a whole bar.

(e) Typical dance rhythms, skipping, tangos, waltzes, gallops, cha cha cha.

These things can be played with, practised, danced, observed, with music, without, with percussion, until rhythmic knowledge is built up cognitively and in competence.

CHAPTER 3

Theme III: Introduction to Space

This is the first Theme in which the focus is not on the moving individual himself but on his environment. A great step forward is made when this Theme is mastered, because space is the medium in which dance takes place, and the mover must be at home in it if he is to fully develop his movement potential and be independent. Music is able to provide the rhythmical flow of some dance, but nothing provides a flow in the space except the dancer's own interest in it.

Spatial awareness comes over a period of years and in a particular sequence. To begin with the space needs to be concrete, in the form of objects which the young dancer can see, or names of things which he knows: floor, window, centre of the room, for example. The visual part of his perceptual equipment provides the information which he needs in order to line himself up with his environment. Later, the space becomes filled by shapes (*see* Theme IX), i.e. things he knows visually become linked to movements felt kinesthetically. Later, the space becomes abstractly organised in logical divisions (*see* Theme XI) which are understood cognitively and perceived, by oneself kinesthetically, and by others visually.

1. USING THE SPACE

In order to transform the void, which is space, into matter to be danced with, a theme imagining this is presented first.

With older pupils, able to relate to the abstract idea of space, this play theme can be omitted.

The body can *explore* the space, the gestures creating havoc amongst the dust particles in it or moving through it carefully, hardly disturbing them. The attention throughout is centred on the space and what it means to dance and move in it. The body can *penetrate* the space by diving into it, extending the limbs into it; the body becomes a column directed into different places all around it. The body can generally *fill* the space, by leaping and spreading, the limbs gesticulating all round to sweep every particle of space to different places, parts of the body simultaneously reaching out and finding new places to move in. The attention is constantly changing from place to place when the body is filling the space, while when penetrating it, all energies are concentrated on the one spot, towards which the movement flows. The body can *surround* the space and *repulse* it. In the former the body gathers a chosen part of the space in towards itself, embracing it with arms, legs, trunk and head, which can work together with a common focus or can each have their own chosen areas. In a repulsing movement the space is pushed away gently or with force, as if separating the body from it.

2. SPATIAL AREAS

The focus can be on certain areas of the space, just as it can be on parts of the body. There are three fundamental areas: one which is *high* up and above, another *deep* and beneath, and a third, between these two, which is on a *medium* level and around the body. For the young child, high is ceiling-wards, deep is floorwards, and medium is wallwards. The symbols for these areas are:

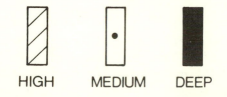

HIGH   MEDIUM   DEEP

One can move into these levels and the arrival in a new area takes the body into a new situation. These situations need to be sensed kinesthetically and achieved bodily. The deep level can be experienced by bending the knees fully, kneeling, sitting, lying and crouching. Many combinations of supports can be used, including knees and elbows, shoulders and head. The high level can be experienced by leaping and jumping, reaching upward while on the toes, balanced on one foot or two. The medium level can be experienced by reaching out around the body, stepping out and leaning well into the level so that the horizontal nature of it is felt and performed.

To go from the low into the high level is a rising movement. The reverse is a lowering movement with arrival in the deep area. These two areas are bordered by the ceiling and the floor while the middle level has four facets, the walls. If one stands in the centre of the room one can appreciate the four areas, *in front, behind, to the right* and *to the left*. These, together with *above* and *below*, make the six basic spatial areas around the body.

Three strands of learning are available here; first the acquisition of the ability to move the body into the levels and the areas, movements which require some strength, and technical achievement; secondly, the sensing of these changes as quite distinct ways of moving; thirdly, the notion of appropriateness to a dance being created or viewed of the choice of area and the manner of performing it.

Theme I and Theme II provide the foundation on which these new spatially oriented movements can be built. The teacher may deal with spatial aspects isolated from dynamics and action to begin with, but space is a medium in which dancing takes place and by which dancing becomes ordered. The objective is to achieve a *dynamic body in space*.

3. BODY ZONES

The body has a sphere of space around it in which it moves. Each person has his own sphere which is related to him only; this is termed the *kinesphere*. The *general space* is all that is beyond the body's reach. All that is within range is the personal kinesphere of each individual which is carried with him as he travels through the general space.

Parts of the body have their own zones within the kinesphere, being these parts of space which each part of the body can encompass without involving adjacent parts. The arms and legs have their own zones. The arms naturally fill the upper area with their gestures while the legs occupy the lower. The dancer will experience this natural use of space and also try the more exacting task of inversion, by reaching out into the zones which are not immediate and feeling the accompanying movements of the centre of the body which are necessary to achieve this. It is just this penetration into the arm zones which sends the legs beating up, propelling the body into the air, and the invasion of the arms into the leg zone that leads the spine to bend and arch. Using the zones of the left limbs by the right limbs introduces crossing-over movement into the vocabulary.

The spatial areas and the body zones are the same places looked at from two different perceptual points of view. Spatial areas divide the environment, body zones bring consciousness of the body in the divided environment.

Vocabulary building, technical achievement, opportunity for daring, and increased sensitivity are offered in this Theme, together with another avenue into kinesthetic knowing.

4. EXTENSION IN SPACE

As the limbs bend and stretch, they move towards the edge of the kinesphere, and towards the central part of the body. The intention of these movements is given a new meaning in this Theme, by attending to the change of focus from "out" to "in". Stretching out, with focus far away, becomes extending into space. Bending in, with focus near, becomes contracting into the body. The *focus* changes from self to outside to self again. From these arise two states, *far* from the body and *near* to the body, which are usually accompanied by outward and inward focus. The trunk can extend into space. It feels long and pulled out. The face may be turned to focus on the direction of the extension, or the top of the head be the leading surface.

Older students are also able to master an extended movement which has an inward focus towards the body centre, or a contracted movement with focus on the space, i.e. outward. Counter-tensions arise because of the conflict that is caused by the simultaneous outward and inward pull. The simplicity of going outward and inward both physically and with focus is a marked contrast to this duality.

As the body extends into space it becomes "large" and as it comes into the centre it becomes "small". These are the *elementary body shapes* (*see* Theme IX, 4). Small children love to play between being small and being large. They can do this slowly, as if growing, or abruptly as if giving someone a surprise. All kinds of growing and shrinking plays which result in shapes can be made.

Concentration on the spatial aspect of extending helps youngsters to achieve long lines in their stretched legs, bodies and arms. This feels good to do and looks good to see. This ability provides one of the essential qualities which distinguishes dancers from other movers, for it provides a statement of the dancer's mastery of the boundaries of his spatial medium.

5. SPACE WORDS

There are many words which help to stimulate movement with a spatial bias. These are mostly prepositions. The following is a list which might prove useful and can be supplemented by the teacher and the class:

over, under, on to, into, above, below, through, towards, away from, near, far, close to, via, around, up against.

Children enjoy interpreting such words. The teacher may choose three, such as through, over, and around, and ask the children to dance them in any order that they wish. A partner can then watch and see if he can tell which order has been used. The words can be chosen so that easily discernible movement results and the teacher can later take words which are more alike, such as into and on to, which require much more careful movement interpretation.

6. BASIC SPATIAL ACTIONS

An introduction to dimensional movement can be given early on in movement training, although this is not really dealt with in any depth until Theme XI. The dimensions are:

up-down, right-left, forward-backward.

The actions resulting from movements into these directions are:

rising, falling, opening, crossing, advancing, retreating.

These actions can be orientated to the parts of the room, especially when the pupils are younger. Older pupils will be able to perceive the directional actions without concrete points of reference. These movements are ways of co-ordinating the steps and gestures of the body through spatial constraints. The contrast in the co-ordination of the spatial actions provides six kinesthetic sensations which are basic to dancing. They can be practised for achievement, looked for in choreographies, or used as vocabulary enrichment. Ultimately, a dynamic body dancing in space is the objective which is begun in Theme III.

CHAPTER 4

Theme IV: The Flow of the Weight of the Body in Space and Time

1. CONTINUITY

The first and simplest strand of the flow factor is called continuity. It is not descriptive of the quality of each movement but of the fact of the way movements follow each other. If the movement is *continuous*, without starts and stops, it has continuity and is loosely said to be flowing on. If the movements stop and start, the sequence is discontinuous. It is said not to be flowing on, but to be *interrupted*.

The attention here is on how movements follow on from one another, the transitions between each movement. Adjustment may be made in order to prepare for the next action during the completion of the first one. Thought may have to be on the next move in order to achieve the transition in kinesthetic sensing, and control of these transitions is the meat of this Theme.

2. BODY FLOW

The second strand is concerned with the way the movement flows through the body. It flows *successively* through the body if the activity can be seen and felt to pass from one body part to another adjacent part in succession. It flows *simultaneously* throughout the body if the activity can be seen and felt to happen in all the moving body parts at the same time. As an example: moving from a curled position near the floor to a stretched position upwards; with simultaneous flow, the hands, head, knees and spine will all start moving together and continue moving together and all will reach the ending position at the same time; with successive flow, the knees could start first, then in a sequential way the spine, head, arms and finally fingers, so that one part after another begins and each part arrives at the final position at different times. These two methods of moving can be included in vocabulary acquisition and in play situation.

There are particular sequences of successive body flow which are useful to practise:

(a) Shoulder, elbow, wrist, fingers, and the reverse. This flow can be used in a figure of eight shape, or in opening and closing with rotation of the arms in and out, or flowing within a position as an undulation. Each movement can be done in three ways:

(i) in the sequence indicated;

(ii) in the reverse order;

(iii) with simultaneous flow.

(b) Hip, knee, foot. Leg gestures often use this body flow. Any combination of forward and sideways directions can be used, and the rotation of the limb will vary according to the direction chosen. In gestures across the body, inward rotation is necessary, and in open gestures outward rotation. Hip-knee-foot succession is not possible for backward directions, but can lead well into steps in all other directions.

(c) Knee, hip, chest, head. Successive flow through the body in this sequence results in a body wave. This can be done symmetrically, in which case each part moves towards the direction forward-high. The arms can either accompany with a movement downward to forward to upward, or move contrary to the wave, scattering backwards away from the body. This wave can be done asymmetrically, to either side or diagonally sideways, in which case it is easier to let the arms accompany the body. These are only a few of the ways in which knee, hip, chest, head flow can be used, as any position can be the starting or finishing point for such successive movements.

(d) Less usual sequences can be used, e.g. left knee, right hip, right shoulder, right elbow, head.

(e) Hand movements can be practised in both forms of body flow so that the fingers can move in unison or sequentially.

Successive and simultaneous flow can be combined with actions, with a variety of dynamics, in large and small movements, and in air and on the floor, they can be technically acquired, discovered for vocabulary, observed in other people, and incorporated in compositions.

3. FREE AND BOUND FLOW QUALITIES

Laban explains *free flow* as follows (*see Modern Educational Dance* by Laban):

> "In an action in which it is difficult to stop the movement suddenly, the flow is free."

He explains *bound flow* as follows:

> "In an action capable of being stopped and held without difficulty, at any moment during the movement, the flow is bound."

Free flow can also be described as "fluent", "uncontrolled", "abandoned", "going", "wholehearted", "outpouring".

Bound flow can also be described as "careful", "controlled", "restrained", "stopping", "cautious", "limited", "withheld".

This strand of flow is concerned with the way in which the movement is controlled or not controlled.

Controlling a movement may result in stopping it, altering it, or adjusting it. Stopping it does not always, by any means, entail causing it to stop altogether. What stops is the natural completion of the movement in question, and in its place another movement may occur, probably a correction of the one interrupted.

In all cases, the control is caused by the intake of information which demands a change of some kind. This information has three main sources. The first source is the body's own senses. The mover sees, or hears, or senses, or feels that an error is being made or is about to be made, and corrects it. At the moment of preparing to correct, the flow of the movement is *bound*. The second source is the body's own memory. The mover remembers that, in this situation before, something occurred which required alteration. In remembering, the movement becomes cautious and bound. The third source is emotional, or chemical, either actual emotion or virtual emotion (pretended). The mover feels unhappy, frustrated, unloving, nervous, and generally anti the movement. The feeling causes the movement to become bound. In a behavioural situation these feelings may be real, but in dance they are simulated (Langer S. K. 1952).

Free flow movement occurs when the mover is not expecting information of the kind which requires correction or arrest, and the natural rhythm of the movement flows on in an unguarded manner. The perceptual processes are not at the ready, the memory is providing encouraging information, and the feelings are of enjoyment and satisfaction.

There are of course many instances where the flow is neither bound nor free. There is neither enjoyment nor caution, simply action, there is no over-alertness to cues nor ignoring of cues but simple acceptance of cues and appropriate action.

The static tension mentioned in Theme II under Weight Qualities is sometimes confused with bound flow. Bound flow may produce examples of static tension, but static tension need not be bound. One way of controlling or of anticipating the need to control is to use static tension. This is simply one way of doing it; another is to slow down, another is to waver, another is to contract.

During the learning of a given sequence or a dance, particularly a difficult one, the flow will begin by being interrupted and bound, because the teacher will provide information which requires the pupils to adjust what they are doing to conform to the prescribed patterns. Gradually, as the cues become known, the boundness will diminish. What takes its place is the flowless condition of efficient movement. Over and above this may come the free and bound qualities which provide the (simulated) feeling. The continuum from restrained to abandoned, withheld to outpouring, colours the dance. Dances with flow qualities are much more exciting to do than those without them, and they are also more interesting to watch. However, flow can be overdone. The result is self-indulgent and aesthetically impoverished.

4. FLEXIBLE AND DIRECT SPACE QUALITIES

Movements in space follow straight lines, curving lines, twisting lines. They make circles, figures of eight, doodles, and all manner of patterns. These are facts about the use of space which can be seen as a continuum from straight and linear to twisting and plastic. In conjunction, one has a response to the available space which is either restrictive or indulgent; one either limits the use of space to conform with patterns decided upon, or one lavishly expands in space around the patterns decided upon. These two strands combine to provide the two basic space qualities of direct and flexible which are the poles at either end of the continuum.

A *direct* movement can be described as "straight", "keeping strictly to the path or to the point". In order to retain a non-deviating path the attention must be kept directly on the place of arrival or points passed through during a curve. It is a restricted use of space. No importance is felt for the space that is left on either side of the pathway of the action.

A *flexible* movement can be described as "roundabout", "wavy", "undulating", "plastic", "deviating", "indirect". It is a movement which wanders through the space, several parts of the body going into different places at the same time. It is not an aimless wander which would have a passive attitude, but an enjoyment of using the space to the full. It is generous in attitude towards the space and indulges in it.

Successive body flow has an affinity with flexibility, and simultaneous body flow with directness. However, in dance, where the natural flow of movement is tempered by aesthetic criteria, and a wide vocabulary is allowable, flexibility may be seen with simultaneous body flow, and directness with successive body flow.

Central and peripheral body guidance distinguishes between movements which begin in the centre of the body and movements which are led by the peripheral parts of the body, hand surfaces and feet. Flexibility has affinity with central guidance, and directness with peripheral guidance but again, in the art form, any combinations may appear.

Focusing and looking, visual alertness, is linked with the spatial qualities. Flexible focusing occurs when the eyes pass over the space, the environment and the things and people in it, possibly searching. Direct focusing occurs with straightforward visual concentration.

The fact that the limbs and trunk can and do rotate or twist alters the patterns made in space. Flexibility is often manifest in twists while directness is not. But again this may not be so in the art form of dance, where affinities are deliberately ignored.

The two poles of the continuum appear then as:

Flexibility = twisted pattern, plastic, central guidance, successive body flow, sliding focus, twisting limbs and trunk, indulgent control.

Directness = straight pattern, linear, peripheral guidance, simultaneous body flow, concentrated focus, no limb and trunk twists, restrictive control.

As this is a continuum, one will expect to find all manner of movements, or moments in movements, which are in between these two. It is not very profitable to try to identify all these in-between stages. The important point is to gain a concept of the space quality continuum, and how it affects the use of the body.

There will, as with all the motion factors, be many instances where the spatial qualities are irrelevant, either because no particular effort is being made to control the space or because other elements, such as strength, or suddenness, or free flow, are swamping the receipt of spatial sensations in the kinesthetic sense network.

5. THE FOUR MOTION FACTORS AS CONTINUUMS

This completes the explanation of the four motion factors Weight, Time, Space, and Flow. Each is concerned with the action and the attitude of the moving person. Laban attempted to identify out of this immensely complicated interplay of the four factors, those basic elements which are the poles on four continuums (Laban R. 1947 *Effort*). It is as if he identified black and white as the poles on that continuum. Everyone knows that shades of greys are seen and made. It is pointless to look at each grey and ask, "Is this black or white?". It is equally pointless to look at a movement and say, "Is this movement flexible or direct?".

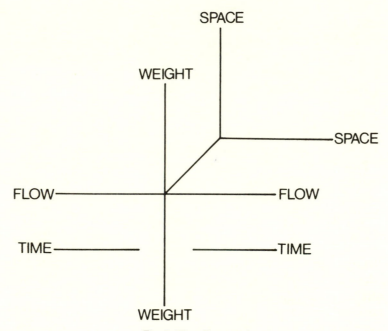

Fig. 2. *The effort graph.*

What can be identified is that the grey is on the black/white continuum and not the yellow/red continuum, that the grey is blacker here than there or whiter in this corner than that corner. What can be identified in a movement quality here is that it is on the flexibile/direct continuum, not the strong/light continuum, and one can decide on the increase or decrease of the flexibility at certain points in the movement.

The poles of the four continuums are identified in symbol form as follows:

WEIGHT   TIME   SPACE   FLOW

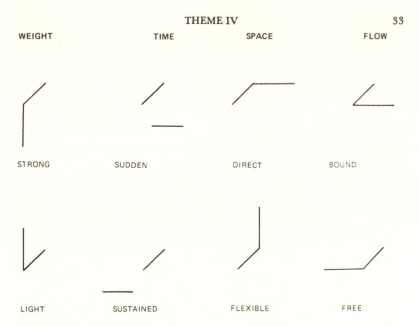

STRONG   SUDDEN   DIRECT   BOUND

LIGHT   SUSTAINED   FLEXIBLE   FREE

Notice that the words "moment in the movement" have been used throughout, rather than "movement". This is because dance movements do not remain in one quality throughout, unless specifically so choreographed. They are rhythmic and constantly changing along one continuum or another. The moments in the movements which are strong, light, sudden, sustained etc., can be identified, and what goes on in between is the general flow of the movement, unidentifiable at this stage. This identification of moments is very important, as it builds up the concept of dynamics in dance. The accurate and sensitive performance of these moments is also important, as it builds up the skill of dynamics in dance. The versatile and imaginative play with these moments is also important as it builds up the confidence in the medium of movement, towards its use creatively in composition. All occur in movement of any kind, but the stress may be placed on just one factor, such as Time, or two factors, such as Weight-Space, or three factors, such as Weight-Space-Time. Combinations of the qualities of the two motion factors of Weight and Time have been dealt with in Theme II, and in this Theme other possible combinations are made as follows.

(a) Flow-Space;   *(d)* Weight-Space;
(b) Flow-Time;   *(e)* Space-Time.
(c) Flow-Weight;
This makes six combinations in all.

When the three motion factors of Space, Weight and Time are combined, the movement is called an *Effort Action.* These are dealt with in Theme VII.

6. TWO-MOTION-FACTOR QUALITIES

Weight-Time combinations have been described in Theme II. Their symbols are:

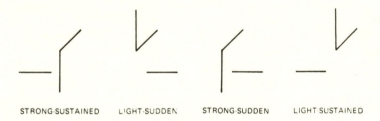

STRONG-SUSTAINED   LIGHT-SUDDEN   STRONG-SUDDEN   LIGHT-SUSTAINED

The other combinations follow here. The treatment is to give a very broad description of what the moments in the movements may feel like and look like when two motion factors are evident, to facilitate identification (*see also* North M. 1972).

(a) Flow-Space continuum.

(i) Flexible-free, producing all manner of undulating, twisting, turning, winding movements of a fluent and unrestricted nature.

(ii) Flexible-bound, producing twisting, turning, screwing movements with a knotted and restricted nature.

(iii) Direct-free, producing straight, linear, aimed movements which are fluent and unrestricted, which may have a feeling for distance and infinity.

(iv) Direct-bound, producing straight, linear and aimed movements which are limited, restricted and controlled.

The symbols for the Flow-Space poles are:

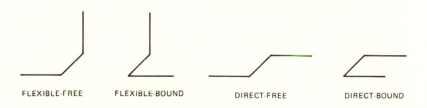

FLEXIBLE-FREE   FLEXIBLE-BOUND   DIRECT-FREE   DIRECT-BOUND

(b) Flow-Time continuum.

(i) Sudden-bound, bringing about jerky disjointed movements of all kinds, spurts of action which stop suddenly.

(ii) Sudden-free, producing bouncy movements, sudden movements which rebound.

(iii) Sustained-bound, producing cautious movements, stalking and slow-motion.

(iv) Sustained-free, producing indulgent lazy movements which feel endless and unhurried.

The symbols for the Flow-Time poles are:

SUDDEN-BOUND   SUDDEN-FREE   SUSTAINED-BOUND   SUSTAINED-FREE

(c) Flow-Weight continuum.

(i) Strong-bound, bringing about cramped movement with great tension.

(ii) Light-bound, bringing about delicate movement with great care taken so that the tension is not too great.

(iii) Strong-free, bringing about vigorous expansive movement.

(iv) Light-free, bringing about airborne buoyant movements.

Heaviness can also be used with free flow, but bound flow induces static tension to appear.

The symbols for the Flow-Weight poles are:

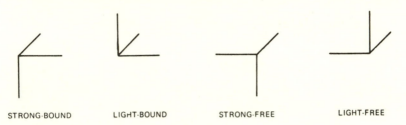

STRONG-BOUND   LIGHT-BOUND   STRONG-FREE   LIGHT-FREE

(d) Weight-Space continuum.

(i) Strong-flexible, producing strong twisting moments, lithe and sinuous.

(ii) Strong-direct, producing strong and aimed moments, downright and solid.

(iii) Light-flexible, producing roundabout moments with fine touch, gently twisting.

(iv) Light-direct, producing gentle moments, threading, and linear.

Heaviness can also be used in flexible and direct moments. The symbols for the Weight-Space poles are:

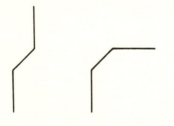

LIGHT-FLEXIBLE   LIGHT-DIRECT

STRONG—FLEXIBLE   STRONG-DIRECT

(e) Space-Time continuum.

(i) Direct-sudden, producing pouncing, pointed, spiky, sharp moments.

(ii) Direct-sustained, producing smooth, linear actions, of a long duration.

(iii) Flexible-sudden, producing twirling, twisted moments, which are indirect, quick and of short duration.

(iv) Flexible-sustained, producing stirring and twisting actions with twists of long duration.

The symbols for the Space-Time poles are:

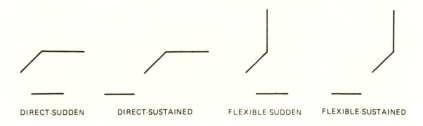

DIRECT-SUDDEN   DIRECT-SUSTAINED   FLEXIBLE-SUDDEN   FLEXIBLE-SUSTAINED

While all these combinations of two motion factors can be performed separately and in succession, it is very difficult to do so. Using these combinations as conscious starting points for movements is not a successful way into dance. They are dynamic colourings of dance, and *the dancing needs to be there before the colouring takes place*. Therefore a return to Themes I–III for actions with body, and spatial vocabulary, will produce the outline which can then be coloured dynamically.

Alternatively, dancing stimulated by quite other starting points, music, ideas, studies, etc., can be appreciated by finding out which continuums are being used, how and when, which preferences dancers habitually have, what combinations constitute the style of a choreographer or ethnic group, and the experience of them enriches the movement vocabulary enormously. Dance-plays can be made with either abstract or dramatic characteristics, and by taking part in these the child is helped to become a versatile mover.

7. PHRASING AND PUNCTUATION

Although there is new work presented in this Theme, its main aim is also to integrate the work of the preceding three Themes. This is done by attending to the phrasing of the movement combinations. Phrases of movement are like

sentences of words, in that a string of words does not necessarily make a sentence and neither does a string of movements. A sentence must contain words which have certain
properties — nouns, verbs, adjectives, adverbs, prepositions,
etc.; it can be a statement, a question or an exclamation, and
so can a movement phrase.

One movement can say much more than one word. For
example, the body carriage can express "the old man with
the hunched back", or "I am curled up near the floor", or "a
proud person with hands on her hips". One can say that the
carriage describes the basic character of the moving person,
the nouns and adjectives. The verbs are the actions such as
running, leaping, sitting, sprawling, and these are qualified
by the quality with which the action is performed, the
quality acting as an adverb. The comparison could go further
but this will suffice to show that movement phrases must
be thought of as part of a language.

A phrase must contain a main action which is done with
clear quality and have either a preparation, a result or both.
Running into a leap and landing could constitute a phrase but
it says too little to be interesting. Much more is said if the
run is speedy, the leap high and asymmetric and the landing
strong and bound, dissolving into light. This is worth saying
because it feels good to do; there is sufficient in it to make
the mover want to participate with his whole being. The
key to this is the flow of the phrase. When movements
follow on from one another in a meaningful way flow is
experienced and it is the presence of flow which increases the
enjoyment of movement. A phrase made up of a direct
movement, a flexible-light movement and three sudden
stamps will not have flow if one movement does not follow
the other in a meaningful way. It could have flow if done
with the directness as a preparation to a flexible and
increasingly light turn which rises, the three stamps being
used to stop the turn. This has flow because it is a sentence
containing actions (verbs) and dynamics (adverbs and
adjectives) and has a preparation-action-result rhythm.

Simple spatial ideas from Theme III can be used as the
subject-matter for simple phrase making. For example,
playing between the three levels, or between big and small

positions, gives scope for expressive movement. The meaning might be: "I am going to reach up and up slowly until I am quite stretched and when I can't stretch any more I am going to fall down and surprise everyone", or, "I am very big and I am shrinking smaller and smaller and smaller until I am in such a tight ball that I must explode". All manner of strong, light, sudden, sustained, direct, flexible, free and bound flow qualities are contained in such phrases so that the aim of integrating earlier themes is possible.

Simple body ideas from Theme I and rhythmic ideas from Theme II can also be used as subject-matter, and later two ideas can be used, for example, emphasis on the elbow with advancing and retreating, or on the feet with strong accents and light accents, jumping and walking with directness and flexibility.

The emphasis all the time in this Theme is on the joining of things together, transitions, appropriateness, beginnings and endings. Older pupils will not attend to phrasing in this play-like way. They will have starting points suitable to their age group, and would be quite unsatisfied by this method. To begin with they will be dancing already, because a vocabulary will have been acquired either in school or out, of some kind. Dances and studies given by the teacher can be looked at from the point of view of transitions. Where transitions were ignored before, now they form the basis for improvement. Where a composition is being undertaken, appropriateness, meaning, startings and endings, dynamic moments, and style selection can be the teacher's emphasis. Analysis of good compositions, perhaps on video, can turn to ways in which dynamics, actions and space are put together in phrases.

Work can be done by looking at the meaning of the phrase from the following point of view: is this like a sentence which ends with a full stop, a comma, a question mark or an exclamation mark? The full stop will make the movement come to a finish in a steady position with finality, the flow will end. The comma means that the stop is not final, the flow will continue into the next phrase which should be on the same subject; the comma says, "Take a breath and continue". The phrase which needs a question mark feels unfinished too and unresolved, in a state of ill-balance. The answer which will solve the query is wanted so the flow is in flux in this kind of sentence. The exclamation mark phrase is fun to do because it says something out of the ordinary and need not follow rules of construction in the same way as a statement.

CHAPTER 5

Theme V: Adaptation to a Partner

In Theme III, the Introduction to Space, the task was to interest the child in focusing his movement on the environment, i.e. the room and the obvious directions, and no longer entirely on himself. In the present Theme the environment becomes another person and some ways of helping the child to become socially adapted in dance are given.

A word is necessary on the relationship between dancing with a partner in the virtual world of art, and communicating non-verbally with a friend in the actual world of everyday (*see* Argyle M. 1967 and Langer, S. K. 1953). The first is simulated and intentional, the second is real and may be intentional or symptomatic. The first has no barriers in the way of what is allowable, while the second has culturally learnt patterns with thresholds beyond which "normal" behaviour does not go. What is bizarre in behaviour may be exciting in art, what is bewildering in behaviour may be moving in art. This Theme has to build a bridge between the two worlds for youngsters.

With young children the transference of attention from self to another child is a great step forward and takes time. Looking at another moving being with interest and finding out that doing things together is fun, are the key steps; the new idea is that special things can be done in dance together which could not be done alone.

It is always fun to do something with somebody else and one of the aims of Theme V is to provide opportunity for this in dance experiences. The give and take and ideas

presented by the presence and actions of the other person
provide the situation that brings about a new experience.
Learning to talk with another person requires rules of
behaviour towards that person which are gradually seen to be
profitable.

In dancing with one another the first golden rule is,
"Watch your partner all the time". This sounds obvious but
it is an idea which cannot be put into practice easily. This is
quite natural when one gives a thought to the senses which
are employed in making and appreciating art forms generally.
Music is aural throughout. But a dancer *feels* himself moving
and has a kinesthetic awareness, while his audience *sees* what
he does. This duality is unique to movement, dance and
mime, and has even led to some doubts that dance should
ever be watched. The onlooker cannot fully appreciate the
muscular-nervous experience of the performer but only the
shapes and patterns, so that the dynamics and qualities of
the movement are seen as if in shadow with the patterns
high-lighted.

It can be clearly seen through the history of dance that
in the periods when rhythmic intricacies and dynamic power
and versatility were at their height, as in the primitive and
Greek era, dance was not usually performed before spectators
but done by everyone with either a ritualistic or recreational
purpose. In other eras, when the theatrical or watching aspect
predominated, the shapes and patterns far outshone the
dynamics. Nineteenth-century ballet is an example of this.
This may in part explain why full appreciation of another's
movement meaning is not as easy as it may at first appear,
and why the cultivation of an acute observation is to be
encouraged, not only because it will help people to dance
together more sensitively but because the awareness of
another person's sensory and nervous happenings, as
manifested in movement, brings a far keener understanding
of him as a being.

1. DOING THE SAME

"Anything you can do I can do." The idea of copying is a
natural one and children like to do it. But it is not as easy as

it seems. To do exactly the same needs precise observation and a high degree of kinesthetic awareness in order to transfer the sight into identical action. The task of the teacher is to awaken the child's powers of observation gradually and this can be methodically done.

(a) *The shape* can be seen and copied as a statue; both are tall and thin, both broad, curled up, twisted or spread out, one child leading, the other watching and then doing.

(b) *The level* of the dance can be the same; both high and then both low. A little phrase of high-low-high can be seen and copied. The movements will not be exactly the same but the important part, i.e. the level, must be.

(c) *The quality* can be copied; for example, a phrase of firm-energetic or light-flowing movement. Not only must the child concentrate on what the other is doing in order to be able to do it himself but the active child will soon learn that he must be very clear. It is no good doing just any movements, they must be recognisable and well performed. The teacher has to see that both children realise where their responsibilities lie in order to make a success of the play. All the qualities in Theme II can be used, at first one at a time and then as a phrase; for example, starting lightly and crisply and finishing firmly and smoothly.

(d) *The rhythm* can be repeated by the partner. According to the age of the dancers, the rhythmic phrases will have varying degrees of complexity. They can be either metric or non-metric. At a simple level, the phrase might be three staccato movements, ta ta ta; later one movement can be made more important, ta ta *ta*, by being bigger and stronger. Ta ta-te *ta* would be a further development. In non-metric rhythms gradual acceleration of beats into a climax, or a long drawn out movement followed by two presto beats, serve as examples. The non-metric phrase is more natural to the young child while the older children like the preciseness and regularity of metre. It must also be remembered that a few people are arhythmic and will have difficulty with metre but will be able to enjoy non-metric rhythms. Again, the movements will not be exactly the same but the important part, i.e. the rhythm, must be.

(e) *The active part of the body* can be observed and a

dance sequence made with the same parts predominating; for example, a stepping and jumping phrase where the legs are obviously the most important part. This can be developed so that particular parts of the leg are clearly seen and felt as leading, such as the toes or knees. A phrase with first feet, then elbows and finally chest would be a further development, more exacting both to perform and to observe.

(f) *Total imitation* is possible, with the ability to imagine the feelings as well as the shapes of the partner. This involvement in another person's kinesthetic feeling is the special way in which dancers communicate with each other.

2. CONVERSATIONS IN MOVEMENT

Having mastered the art of watching a partner and then copying, the next step is to watch and then make a reply, thus establishing a relationship. In "Doing the Same" this was not important, the reply was simply "I see you dancing and now it is my turn". It now has to mean, "I see you dancing to me and I then answer you with my dance". The movements take on a new significance.

(a) *The shape* of the partner's position can indicate the next move. A grows up tall and thin; B lets his movement follow the line from the feet to the tips of A's fingers and continues by jumping away and curling into a ball. A makes a circling movement round the ball and then spreads himself out very wide, and so on, the final position of the partner always being the stimulus to the new phrase.

(b) *The level* of the movements is no longer high, low or medium but "above", "below" and "on the same level with". A can make a phrase which ends above B and B can answer by moving low down below the watching A who can then jump up and end on the same level.

(c) *The quality*. Here there are many possibilities. For example A's quick and lively question may produce a similar answer in B or B may wish to reply in a contrasting manner. The operative word here is "wish". Each child must try to make his own movements speak so that the other person feels he must say something in return. A dramatic situation usually arises. For example, energetic movements tend to become aggressive; slow-powerful ones hypnotic; sharp-crisp ones tantalising; slow-quiet ones calming. When the children concentrate on what their partner is doing these relationships arise. The phrases usually start by being of the same length and gradually, as the two become immersed in what they are doing, the phrases become of irregular length and finally the two children find themselves moving at the same time, the one leading the other in an interchange.

(d) The metre. Older children and adults can sometimes be brought to this state of interchange via metric rather than free rhythm, the security of the beat giving them a framework in which to improvise. For example, taking an eight-beat phrase in moderate tempo, A can make a rhythmic question on 1, 2, 3, 4, B can reply on 5—8. Brief movements, pauses, sustained movements, jumps, turns, etc., can be used and either very simple or intricate rhythms. Simpler rhythms give the best results because the concentration can then be primarily on speaking to the partner and not on making interesting metric inventions. The metre is really only to serve as a duration framework for quality play, and as the interchange begins to interest the two parties, the metre is often abandoned and free rhythm takes its place.

(e) Parts of the body. A's phrase can be directed or finished towards B's feet, enticing him to move them. B dances with his feet and encourages A to answer with the knees or hips or any other part he indicates, either head, arms or tummy, for example. There is no need for a change every time. The partners can have a dance between them with the arms predominating, passing the movement over from one to the other by the finger tips, palm, wrist, etc.

The method described in this Theme has been trial and error, and improvising on the movement ideas together. Further ideas might involve:

(a) proximity to and distance from;
(b) focusing on or away from;
(c) front to, back to, side to;
(d) parallel lines with.

The method could be quite different. Examples of simple duo phrases could be taught and learnt and danced to the other class members. Sculptural figures could be used as examples, two musical instruments as examples, two percussive sounds one after the other.

3. DANCING TOGETHER

Having mastered the art of communicating with another in question and answer form, the next step is to dance at the same time. It has been shown how this naturally follows when the conversation is started on a rhythmic basis. The whole point of dancing together is to create something which an individual could not do on his own. Something that could not be done alone means either an activity with a common purpose, or activity arising out of the need to move because of the presence or actions of the other person. It is so easy for a teacher to fall into the routine, "Do it by yourselves, do it with a partner, and now do it as a group". This kind of approach skims over the surface of relationships, with the result that the children miss far more enjoyable and realistic activities. By realistic is meant "concerned with the real person", the process of realising the potential within people.

It will be found that all beginners tend to dance very close to their partner. Young children feel that the way to make themselves clear is to dance under the other's nose, which is, of course, a great mistake, partly because it is often unpleasant and partly because the partner is only aware of a melee of arms and eyes and cannot possibly distinguish what the over-eager child is trying to say. *Proximity and relationship are not synonymous* and the following can be used to aid this difficulty.

Towards and away or *meeting and parting* is a universal dance pattern, clearly seen in all couple dances. *Approaching* can have many expressions, being done with fine touch or firmly, sudden-directly or in a roundabout way, thus giving a tentative, overwhelming, straightforward or surreptitious expression. Particular parts of the body can lead the approach, for example the finger tips, the back, one side and then the other. Patterns can be used and levels or rhythms according to the wishes of the partners. After the approach, the following can happen: *meeting, passing by, avoiding* by going around one another, *clashing* by contrasting movements, *merging* by the unison quality of some aspect of the movements; all these actions create either concord or deadlock. Finally the partners either stay together or *part*. Many folk dances can be seen to be a mixture of these happenings. Sir Roger de Coverley is a very clear example of meet, merge, part, meet, avoid, part, approach and retire. To the young child the three ideas, "I can come towards you, I can go away from you, and I can go around you", are enough to overcome the tendency to crowd.

Other relationships could be:

(a) looking at;
(b) looking away from;
(c) touching;
(d) surrounding;
(e) bearing the weight of;
(f) sliding under;
(g) jumping over;
(h) going through a gap made by.

Dancing with another person is a fundamental activity. It is sensitising to the ability to empathise with people as people and as dancers. It is applicable to all ages, except the very young.

4. DANCING TO A PARTNER

Dancing "with" and dancing "to" highlight one of the fundamental differences between the art of dancing and the art of communicating (*see* Humphrey D. 1959 and Hayes E. R. 1955). Where both parties are active participants, mutual adaptations can be made, mutual imagination and response. Where one is active and the other a recipient, as an audience, the onus for the effectiveness of the movement is on the active dancer. Immediately new constraints and initiatives need to be made. The dance, or phrase, will acquire a "front" directed to the watcher. Every movement will be seen from that view and from that distance. Periods of pause between phrases while the other replies will now be seen as visibly held positions. Starts, ends, floor patterns, focus, body placement, all take on new significance. Selection has to be made.

The next progression in this Theme is to pass from dancing alone to someone, to ' dancing with a partner to someone, dancing a duo. All the previous sub-headings need looking at again in this light. "Watch your partner", but not obviously; learn to dance with him by seeing in peripheral vision rather than focused vision. Copying becomes a major theme, for seeing one movement in two bodies is interesting. Simultaneity and sequentiality of copied movements takes on new dimensions. The sculptural element of the duo in the form of juxtaposing of bodies or volumes with varied shapes and voids and masses becomes the development of "statue making". The distance between the dancers, their orientation, their overlapping, merging, masking, are all now to be seen as significant, visually.

Looking at other people dancing, and learning from that looking, has been mentioned in each Theme. In this Theme it is essential that the looking becomes seeing, that the visually perceptive eye is encouraged to be an active participant in the looking (*see* Arnheim R. 1956). As one sees, one processes the perceptions into conceptions. It is important from an early age that the concepts built up of another moving person are empathetic, sensitive, personalised, for that is the affective stuff of relationships in dance. Looking at the outer form of the movement, or its technical achievement, or its mistakes, or its patterns, is the way in which the non-dancer looks without seeing the person inside. All the dance critics who make loud noises for improved technique and pleasant-looking dance in schools are looking in this way, leaning back with passive, entertainment-seeking eyes. The young want to be taught from the beginning how to look subcutaneously so that they see kinesthetically.

5. APPENDIX: A LINK WITH THEME XIV

The work in this Appendix forms a link between that given in Theme V and Theme XIV and can be introduced gradually to bridge a gap between partner and large group work. There is a gradual development in working with other people which includes increasing the number of people to whom one must adapt. In small groups the actual number makes a great deal of difference to the dance, and work in threes, fours and fives can be introduced and the properties of each discovered.

(a) Trios

Three people make a group which partners do not, and because of this, new kinds of relationships and formations appear. For the first time a circle can be made and the movements can be orientated towards the centre of it, away from, and around the centre. New actions are possible such as *splitting, linking, passing between* and *going through* which are additional to the meeting, parting, etc., actions of the duo. Three is a significant number for human relationships and this is embodied in the term "the eternal triangle". Relationships of two against one and one being pulled in two directions make interesting starting-off points for dance improvisation, and the feeling of being left out adds drama. All manner of variations can be made on linear, triangular and circular formations during a dance and this adds interest fo the performers. Lifts, too, are possible with two supporters, and are exciting to do.

Trios for each other and trios for someone else can be made. The improvisations acceptable for each other will need translating for a discerning audience. The necessary selection and need for good performance of the trio are stimulating challenges to achievement and high standards.

(b) Quartets

The particular attribute of the quartet is that the relationship can change from "we are a group" to "we are two pairs". Because of the even number, people tend to use regular formations when dancing in fours, particularly the square. This is not a very inspiring group shape for dramatic contact but if the relationship of three to one is encouraged far more expressive possibilities are opened. The three can surround the one, can leave him out, be split by him, for example. Three-to-one encourages asymmetric spatial relationships which are typical of dramatic dance, while the two pairs and the foursome give rise to symmetric relationships and are found again and again in folk dance. Dances which contain

a change from one to the other are full of lively possibilities
and should be encouraged.

Again, quartets for each other and quartets for others can
be worked. One person as the outside director may be needed
to help in the selection and orientation and adaptation, or
indeed to work a whole quartet as a choreographer.

(c) Quintets

These have even more variation possibilities than the quartet
and five is an excellent number for a dance. The group can
feel itself a unit in circular and linear formations where
meeting, parting, surrounding, leading and following will
all naturally occur. When the group splits, duos and trios
can be formed or a four-to-one situation arise. What is new to
the five is the "wing" formation, that is group movement
led by the middle person of a line, the two on either side
acting as elongations of the leader's arms, i.e. like wings.
Enclosing in front and behind, V shapes, swooping and
swinging round are all fun to use. The "going through" of
the trio is also good with five; it becomes "we go through the
gaps between you". All manner of changes can be made and
dances using a variety of these possibilities provide an
excellent medium in which to enjoy relationships with other
people and to learn effective ways of composing for five
dancers.

CHAPTER 6

Theme VI: The Instrumental Use of the Body and Technique

This Theme is the second to lay stress on the bodily performance in dancing. It is a progression on the work described in
Theme I. The purpose here is to further the general awareness
gained through Theme I by differentiating movement into
actions which can be recognised and by learning how the
parts of the body have clear roles to play in the mastery of
movement. This is done through looking at the movements
the body can do when acting as an instrument and secondly
by building up a technical vocabulary through the practice
of different actions. There is an attempt to link the
functional instrumental use of the body to dance technique
to avoid the latter becoming meaningless skill acquisition
which it so easily can become.

1. THE MEANING OF INSTRUMENTAL USE
OF THE BODY

Hands are the most obvious parts of the body used daily as
instruments. When we pick up an object we grip with our
hands; they make the action of a pincer or a scoop. These are
instrumental movements, gestures which do something. The
hands can be used as a knife for cutting, as a fork for
pronging, as a spoon for scooping, as a cup for containing,
as a plate for supporting, as a hammer for hitting, etc. The
shape that the hands make shows the nature of the instrument.

Although the hands are the usual parts to become instruments, larger parts or even the whole body can take on that character. For instance, the foot can hammer the floor, the whole arm can scoop or the whole body can slice through the air. When the action is confined to the hands mimetic movement results. When the action is enlarged so that the whole body becomes the instrument the mimetic element dissolves into dance. The action may no longer be recognisable but the movement will have meaning for the performer. For instance, the actions of gripping and releasing can be made mimetically by the hands, articulation being given by the shape that the hands make to indicate the nature of the object held. This can be transferred into the whole body so that the pressure instead of being between finger and thumb, is between arms and chest or thighs and face, the release also being in the whole body. This is no longer a mimetic action but dance.

Gripping consists in gathering the fingers together towards a definite point. The placing of the point can vary in that one can grip from above, below, behind or from the side. In whole body movement, the gripping is the gathering together of the limbs to a certain point, the easiest of which is in front of the body, making the spine round over forwards. Gathering can also be made around a point placed anywhere in the kinesphere, above the head, behind the back, near the feet, far to the side. The releasing action comes as a scattering movement away from the chosen point. These *gathering* and *scattering* movements are typical of dance gestures and can be seen in almost any lyrical dance. They are often performed with the shape of a figure 8, with much arching and rounding of the spine and with jumps and turns.

When dance gestures are inspired by abstract shapes, the result can be meaningless, particularly for beginners, but when they are inspired by the instrumental actions of the body, however far removed from the mimetic original, shapes arise which are full of meaning for the dancer. The study of these instrumental actions therefore forms a vital background to the abstract shapes which will inspire movements later. When these are reached, in Theme IX, their significance will be recognised.

2. THE FIVE BODY ACTIONS AND STILLNESS

The five Body Actions are as follows:

(a) Gesture, which includes all movements of the body which are not concerned with supporting the weight;

(b) Stepping, which includes all transferences of the weight from one support to another;

(c) Locomotion, which includes methods of transporting the body from one place to another;

(d) Jumping, which includes all movements where there is no point of support;

(e) Turning, which includes all movement where a change of the front is made.

One more category of movement is given in this series:

(f) Stillness, which includes all positions of the body.

(a) Gesture

This was introduced in Theme I. Here its gathering and scattering properties and vocabulary potential can be explored and mastered. It may be helpful to analyse gathering and scattering further, from the gestural point of view. Apart from the patterns which these actions make, they are combinations of:

(i) inclining the limbs and trunk;
(ii) twisting the limbs and trunk;
(iii) contracting the limbs and trunk;
(iv) extending the limbs and trunk;
(v) returning them to their normal carriage.

These units of gesture readily synthesise in all manner of combinations. In order that they should not be treated as technically isolated actions, their synthesis in gathering and scattering, slicing, scooping, smoothing, pronging, etc. is mentioned.

Gestures, although instrumentally belonging to the arms, are in dance equally the province of the legs. Here basic controls and variations on leg gestures are taught and learnt, by whatever method is appropriate. Gathering and scattering are clumsy in the legs but their components are not. The special role of "outturn" or "parallel legs" in gestures may be attended to here.

(b) Stepping

This action was introduced in Theme I as weight transference. Vocabulary variety and basic kinesthetic sensing were the aim. Here the stepping is to be experienced as having an intrinsic function in dance, a supporting function. The production of supporting bases for gestures is here explored and practised. High up supports, low down supports, outturned, parallel, wide, narrow, kneeling and sitting are all possible, useful, and require practice, and present meanings and experiences.

(c) Locomotion

Locomotion consists in transferring the weight of the body from one point of support to another in succession. This is usually from one foot to the other but can also be from any part of the body to any other. The main focus is on getting from one place to another and in establishing the point of arrival. The ways of doing this are manifold. Words such as crawling, prancing, creeping, shuffling, sliding, striding, rolling, etc., will provide the class with the stimulus for inventive methods of travelling. Children find imitation of mechanical forms of locomotion amusing to try out. All kinds of running and walking should be practised, using backwards and sideways directions as well as forwards, and all kinds of rhythmical combinations. The young child is full of ideas and invention within this framework, while the older child may not like rolling and crawling but may prefer stepping and running as the normal method of getting from place to place.

Weight bearing and travelling on unusual parts of the body is not only a child's play activity as might at first be thought. Because it is the reversal of the natural it can be very expressive, particularly of the extraordinary, the exaggerated, the funny, the abnormal or the disturbed. The awareness of these expressions will not necessarily arise while experimenting with supports but a basis will be given for their meaningful use later.

The different forms of locomotion found by using rhythm and quality changes will each produce their own expression. The children can be encouraged to find out the meaning for them of their own invention so that the movement arouses their imagination.

Kinesthetic messages are received and processed into concepts. Here the messages about locomotion are to be conceptualised in relation to function, expression, experience, and imitative elements. The kinesthetic sense is just as capable of sending messages as any of the other senses. Success in choreography depends on the sensitivity of the kinesthetic sense, just as musical composition depends on having a sensitive ear. The gradual training of the body to be awake to what it is doing is a major part of movement study and should be practised from the start.

(d) Jumping

Jumping is a fundamental part of dancing. Fighting gravity has been an activity of man for centuries and is reflected in his dance.

Gravity is felt as a force acting on the body early on in life, while levity, which is the essence of jumping, requires active and co-ordinated effort, acquired later. It is for this reason that Laban placed work on "Elevation" late in his Sixteen Themes; it is Theme XIII. In the present Theme only the preliminaries of jumping are studied.

Jumping is used instrumentally for bouncing like a ball, flying like an arrow, or releasing into the air like a spring. It is used as an aid to reaching, as a means of getting away from or getting over. Scissor-like and hitting actions may occur in the air.

All jumps are variations of the *five basic jumps*. These are:

(a) from one foot to the same foot;
(b) from one foot to the other foot;
(c) from one foot to both feet;
(d) from both feet to both feet;
(e) from both feet to one foot.

The first jump is a hop, the second a leap but the English language has no words for the last three jumps. Ballet uses the following French terms: *temps levé, jeté, assemblé, sauté* and *sissonne*, and these can be used when the need arises. Combinations of steps and jumps can be tried out and the most common studied, such as the skip, polka or setting. Attention can be drawn to the different nature of jumps in duple and triple time. The former is earthbound and bouncy while the latter has a swing and the jump can be higher. In duple time the stress of invention can be on the variety of landings possible, while in triple time the variety is more readily made by the gestures of the legs in the air.

As in locomotion, thinking about the meaning of the child's invention, the mood or humour of the movement, or the action it portrays, is important. A child's imagination is so much more alive than an adult's that he will very soon find all sorts of meanings for his own or a partner's movement.

Besides invention, vocabulary enrichment, and concept building, there is a skill element here which has to be acquired if mastery of movement is to be achieved. The ability to jump with neat, strong feet, light landings and pliant ankles and knees is an undoubted asset, giving confidence to the dancer that he can include all manner of jumps in his dancing safely, and aesthetically.

(e) Turning
Turning is an important action in the dance. To keep the same front throughout a dance is improbable, if not impossible, and certainly limiting.

Turning is achieved through a combination of gesturing and stepping. Supports for the turn provide the axis around which the turn is made, usually a vertical axis. This axis spins, either supported on one pivoting foot or on two stepping feet. The smaller the pivoting area, the easier it is to get round. Children first try turning with pattering feet, then by spinning on one, which is much harder to achieve, and then by jumping which is increasingly hard with the amount of turn.

Continual turning produces dizziness, and loss of balance. This is part of its magical quality. Down-up movements quickly dispel the dizziness.

Dancers need to be able to turn to the right and to the left equally fluently, although people usually have a preference.

Turns have to be started by gestures, which provide the impetus to go around. A twist in the opposite direction to the turn gives a preparation; unwinding from the twist leads into the turn. Opening and closing, leg and arm gestures initiate turns by providing the impetus. An open step prepares a closing turn; a crossing step prepares an opening turn. Rising and sinking while turning results in spiralling. Positions may be held throughout a turn, or positions appear and dissolve during the turn. The skill element in turning can be attended to in this Theme, as well as the instrumental use.

(f) Stillness

Stillness is primarily a question of the flow of movement and is therefore rightly considered first in Theme IV as it is fundamental as a movement experience and essential as a technical requirement. The use of the body to achieve stillness is considered here.

Balance and the shape that the body makes are two considerations in holding a position. Both arise from consciousness of the relation between different parts of the body, but the motivation behind each is different. When trying to balance, the gravity line and the counter pull of the limbs are felt as spokes related to the hub, the body centre. When thinking of the shape that is being made, the relationship is felt between one spoke and another. The attention is often not on the body at all but on the shape of the space left between the limbs. The latter, thinking of stillness in terms of shape, is not dealt with at this stage but comes in Theme IX. Here, the concern is to increase the ability to balance by feeling the muscular tension necessary to achieve and hold the position.

A child finds it difficult to balance on one leg, particularly when the other leg is far off the floor. The teacher can help by starting with swaying movements, getting the child to feel the moment when he is just between safe and toppling over. This can be done sideways, forwards and backwards and with a diagonal base. The same thing can be done with rising on the toes. The tension in the free leg must be felt and that of

the muscles in the hip region. The swaying can increase in
size so that the trunk participates. Unless the relationship
between the leg, the spine and head is felt, the child will
overbalance. The cultivation of this awareness in the class
is the job of the teacher so that stillness can be achieved at
will and with certainty.

3. COMBINATIONS OF THE FIVE BODY ACTIONS

They are:

    (a) gesturing while stepping;
    (b) stepping or weight transference during locomotion;
    (c) travelling while turning;
    (d) turning jumps;
    (e) gestures during jumps;
    (f) gestures and locomotion;
    (g) travelling jumps;
    (h) step jump rhythms;
    (i) stepping during turns;
    (j) turns with gestures.

Some of these have already been included in the text, but
(c) (d) and (g) are new and should be used as a progression
on what has gone before.

Further studies of specific techniques would be in place
here. Not all are written about adequately, but books and
films would help to give some idea if a trained teacher is
not available (see Clarke & Crisp 1973, Cohen 1974, Ellfeldt
1976, Lawson 1960, Nadel & Nadel 1970, Winearls 1968,
Sherbon 1968).

4. SEQUENCES OF ACTIONS

Bodily skill is increased by the practice of sequences con-
sisting of transitions from one body action into another.
The ability to change from one to the other in a skilful
manner contributes to body technique. The task of the
teacher is: (a) to present gradually situations which require
increasingly skilful body use; (b) to help the child to feel how
one action can grow into another, thereby arousing the
child's desire to acquire skilful movement.

The following is an example of *(a)*:

Gathering and scattering gestures on the spot; the same while hopping on one foot and then the other; the second stage while turning a complete turn; then with travelling down the room while turning; lastly, travelling in a circular pathway while performing the hopping-turning motif.

The following is an example of *(b)*:

A preparatory gathering leg and arm gesture, stepping out leading into running, increasing speed into a leap and finally balancing on the leg on which you landed. This sequence will be seen as the gradual building up to a climax followed by control.

Sequences of actions can be stimulated by words which conjure up different uses of the body. The following list of such words may prove useful and can be supplemented by the teacher or the children:

flying, whirling, pouncing, hovering, creeping, dangling, sprawling, darting, twisting, precipitating, falling, shivering, drifting, spinning, tossing, curling, sinking, collapsing, overbalancing, crawling, bowing, rising, opening, closing, bursting, exploding.

The words should have some logical sequence so that the flow of movement is enhanced and not hampered.

CHAPTER 7

Theme VII: Dynamics through the Basic Effort Actions

Theme VII is concerned with further differentiation of the quality in movement and is a progression of Themes II and IV.

When the three motion factors of weight, time and space are clarified within the same movement an articulate action results.

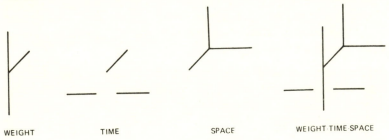

WEIGHT   TIME   SPACE   WEIGHT-TIME-SPACE

There are eight of these weight-time-space actions which are called the basic effort actions. They are given the title "basic" because they form the base from which more subtle qualities are drawn. They may be likened to the primary colours in that other colours are made from them. In dancing, the basic effort actions do not often appear in their undiluted or unmixed form, just as primary colours may not be present in large quantities in a painting. However, the effort actions form recognisable landmarks in the ephemeral rhythm and flow of dance and as such must be identified. This Theme is therefore devoted to the study, experience and mastery of them.

The eight basic effort actions are called thrusting, slashing, floating, gliding, wringing, pressing, flicking, and dabbing.

A word is necessary on the term "action". In everyday movement, particularly in personal interaction, dynamic phrases of a postural or gestural kind are made. These postures and gestures can be called actions, and in this connection effort actions are those gestures and postures which contain clarity in space/time and weight terms. The effort is the action. In dance this is not so, or need not be so. It is much more likely that clear spatial patterns and actions such as jumping, turning, falling will be happening. The effort is the quality of those actions or patterns, and even more likely, the effort is the quality of peaks or important moments only of those actions and patterns.

The names for these effort actions are woefully inadequate, even misleading, but to find adequate ones is a hopeless quest. Context is what provides appropriate meaning, and there are as many contexts as there are movement combinations, and hence more "meanings" than there are words to describe them.

1. THRUSTING AND SLASHING MOMENTS AND MOVEMENTS

These are the same in two respects; they are both strong and suddenly accented. When this movement is projected directly into the space, penetrates it and is aimed, it is called a *thrusting* action:

This goes straight out from the body or in towards it or straight into a position. When it whips up the space around the body and the body twists and turns, it is called a *slashing* action:

The slashing causes the body to leap and whirl round and make jumping-turns; the arms and legs beat the air and the centre of the body twists and arches and feels itself moving plastically. The thrusting causes stamping steps and punching gestures of the arms, the muscles of the body make contractions and grip and feel alert. These actions bring about exhilaration and invigoration. The aim of the thrust and the spatial freedom of the slash make a nice contrast.

It is tiring and unprofitable to dance like this for long periods as the movements become weak and heavy and the firm feeling in the tone of the body is lost. But in short phrases each quality of movement produces an experience which no other activity could.

Making thrusting and slashing movements will not necessarily result in dancing. Dancing requires more than this; it requires that the body acts in space dynamically. The thrusting and slashing are, for dance, adverbs; they must become "thrustingly" and "slashingly", qualifying moments in a dance phrase. They could highlight a jump, or a roll, a fall or an extension. They may occur in a movement of the whole-body-as-a-unit, or they may appear in smaller actions of body parts. The legs, in technical practice, thrust and slash while the rest of the body remains quiet.

Hopefully, a good teacher will only have the words "thrust" and "slash" in the back of his mind and not on the tip of his tongue. He will use words which are more evocative of dance situations, expressions, and feelings. He might use boisterous, riotous, whirling, elated, sword-like, marcato, shooting, blazing, piercing, brutal, pierced, sharp. He can then refer to the space/weight/time components of thrusting and slashing, and clarify the boisterous movements so that they have strong moments, speedy moments and either straight or roundabout moments. And hopefully he will not forget flow, for the boisterous movements may be freely flowing on, one to another, or come to moments of restraint in bound flow.

2. FLOATING AND GLIDING MOMENTS AND MOVEMENTS

These are alike in two respects in that they are sustained and light, i.e. their weight and time qualities are the same. They differ in spatial use, just as in thrusting and slashing.

When the palms and side of the hand lead this sensitive movement and smooth their way through and over the air, coming straight towards and away from the centre or passing the body by, a *gliding* movement is performed.

The movement is flat, without undulations or waves; it is direct; it cuts through the space and is clearly aimed, as is a thrusting action. Serenity, quietness and evenness appear and are felt when gliding is continued over a peried of time. When the wrists, fingers and elbows feel this quality they lead the rest of the body into more roundabout and twisting movements. The spine helps by undulating and waving and the legs by lifting lightly off the ground and supporting the body with careful rising-falling-turning steps. The whole being seems to stir. This is called a *floating* movement:

Floating and gliding are clearly defined because the body has to act differently in order to do them, with particular parts of the limbs and body being more important to each action. They are akin but not the same. They contrast clearly with the two preceding actions' qualities. Thrusting is opposite in action and sensation to floating; one is strongly accented and direct, the other is sustained, light and flexible. Slashing is opposite to gliding. The one is strongly accented and flexible, the other is lightly sustained and direct.

In dancing, floating and gliding actions become adverbs qualifying the verbs of dancing. A soft turn with rounded gestures of free leg and arms followed by an arabesque could be performed with floating and gliding colouring. Working from floating and gliding would never bring about such a turn and arabesque. They need to be there first as dance verbs waiting to be coloured. They could equally be coloured by slash and thrust. Arms move, in dance, "floatingly" and "glidingly" while the lower half of the body may be busy with locomotion or steps and gestures. This is part of the dancer's game of "pretending" to his audience that what he does is easy, and so he tries to look unruffled and unstrained by floating and gliding with his arms and chest.

With floating and gliding at the back of his mind, the teacher's vocabulary might include: elegance, poised, breathing loosely, easily, uplifted, lilting, deviate, hover, embraced, encompass, surrounding, approach, delicately, slight, weak. The "deviating" movement may be analysed or clarified in terms of floating components, so that lightness appears somewhere, flexibility at some point, and sustainment or slowness or deceleration at another moment. And the flow factor will, hopefully, not be ignored.

3. WRINGING AND PRESSING MOMENTS AND MOVEMENTS

These actions are connected with slashing and thrusting in that they are strong. They are also connected with floating and gliding because they are sustained. Pressing and wringing are alike in that they are both firmly sustained. When this quality of firmness is directed into the space by the palms, with force behind it from the shoulders and chest and pelvis, and support from the knees and feet, a *pressing* action results:

The whole body pushes itself outward or pulls itself inward. The palms can lead out into different directions at the same time and the legs take a firm and wide stance as a good base. The body feels controlled and full of power.

When the shoulders and hips take on the sustained strength and move towards and against one another, a *wringing* action occurs:

The arms help by twisting to enhance the shoulder movement, and the legs made a firmly undulating base. The body feels itself screwing and unscrewing, knotting and opening out.

The contrast of flexible and direct action is clearly felt when a wringing movement dissolves into a direct pressing movement. These are tiring qualities to sustain and may be contrasted with flicking and dabbing which give compensation.

When dancing these adverbial qualities qualify whole movements, and individual moments in rhythmical phrases. Strengthening exercises in dance training require to be done "pressingly" with resistance, and "wringingly" when twisting is involved. The earthbound nature of these two efforts limits their occurrence in dance. Low movement and floor work, rolls and changes of support involve wringing. Central tensions and contractions involve pressing. Dramatic roles involving power use these qualities. Practice of pressing and wringing movements will not produce dancing with these

qualities. The dance must come first and be coloured by
them, by referring to the slowness, aim or roundaboutness,
tension, muscular alertness, strength and resistance.

4. FLICKING AND DABBING MOMENTS AND MOVEMENTS

These are quite different from wringing and pressing. They
are light and sudden, delicately accented. Flicking requires
a flexible use of space:

while dabbing requires a direct aim:

Flicking occurs when the hands and feet lead the body
into sparkling action. Little twisting hops and skips, with
fluttering hands and tossing head, bring the whole body into
excited motion. The fingers become alive, scattering and
gathering, and the knees and feet make roundabout gestures
in the air, lightly stepping and springing.

Dabbing occurs when the body darts here and there with
pointed gestures of feet and hands. Elbows and knees shoot
out, eyes open and the body springs into precise action.
Sharp and crisp and aimed describe the feeling of dabbing.

In dancing, these two adverbs abound; especially in lively,
rhythmic, jumping dance. They usually occur in one part of
the body at a time, the other parts accompanying, for
flicking everywhere at once looks messy and muddled.
However, neatly executed foot movements abound, the

upper half remaining poised; speedy head and hand changes abound with simple steps beneath them.

With the words "flicking" and "dabbing" stored for reference only, the teacher will, hopefully, use other words imaginatively to describe these qualities. Perhaps: sparkling, twinkling, brilliant, excited, witty, glittering, bubbly, frothy, effervescent, gaiety, spiky, birdlike, flutter.

Heaviness has not been mentioned in these basic effort actions. They all involve the active use of the body weight. However, heaviness, the passive weight factor, will also occur, although in much less clear actions. They cannot be controlled in the same way as active actions. Four heavy efforts can be discerned. These occur when:

(a) floating and wringing merge into heavy, slow, more or less flexible moments;
(b) slashing and flicking merge into heavy, quick, more or less flexible moments;
(c) pressing and gliding merge into heavy, slow, more or less direct moments;
(d) thrusting and dabbing merge into heavy, quick, more or less direct moments.

There are no technical terms for these. Laban did not consider heaviness under the umbrella of effort action. However, in dance they do occur, and can be seen. Words like fling, swing, collapse, flop, slop, meander might be used as descriptive of this kind of dynamic.

The following shows the properties of the eight basic effort actions:

Action	Time	Weight	Space
thrusting	sudden	strong	direct
slashing	sudden	strong	flexible
floating	sustained	light	flexible
gliding	sustained	light	direct
wringing	sustained	strong	flexible
pressing	sustained	strong	direct
flicking	sudden	light	flexible
dabbing	sudden	light	direct

The mastery of the feel and the look of these eight basic actions is helpful in order to experience and perform clear movement.

When the movement is made with a skilful performance as the primary aim, the action ability of the performer is taxed and trained. When the action is done with the kinesthetic feel as primarily important, the performer's feeling capacities are taxed. But when these two fuse in a sensitive and skilful performance the movement takes on a special character. An effort has to be made to do this and the resulting movement has been technically referred to as "effort". It is this fusion of action and sensation which results in aesthetic experience. It is stressed in all the Themes, whether they are about dynamics, space, action, or relationships.

5. TEACHING EFFORT FOR YOUNG CHILDREN

Young children are content to play with the different effort actions without any further stimulus in the way of dramatic idea or music. The repetition of qualities and the gradual increase in the number of ways in which these can be brought out in the body are exciting for them. It is advisable to work on the effort actions in pairs of opposites so that compensatory quality is given. The stress of the work will be on one quality with the opposite used for balance and recovery. The pairs of opposites are:

(a) Thrusting and Floating;
(b) Slashing and Gliding;
(c) Wringing and Dabbing;
(d) Pressing and Flicking.

For example, when thrusting is the main action to be experienced floating can be brought in to give the body a rest from the energetic actions which will predominate. Similarly thrusting can be used to balance the effort of being lightly sustained which is necessary when floating is the main action. It is easy to see that an energetic quality needs compensation because of the physical exertion, but it should also be remembered that the mental and physical strain of controlling the body in floating actions is also exhausting in quite a different way. The compensatory effort can be experienced as a recovery between each main action or after a series of actions in the main quality. The duration of the phrase of main actions will be about right if it corresponds with the time taken for one complete respiration, and as the rate of breathing of a child is quicker than that of an adult, the movement phrase should be correspondingly shorter. The rate of the repetition of sudden actions should correspond roughly to the heartbeat and again this will vary with the age of the dancer. The size of the body also affects the rate at which a movement is performed, younger children choosing a quicker pace than older people, as there is less weight to shift and a smaller distance to cover.

It is helpful to have a list of words which will conjure up the mood and actions of each effort quality and to use these words to help the children understand the kind of expression that each contains.

Percussion instruments make an excellent accompaniment to effort actions and each instrument has a quality of sound which will help particular ones. Most schools have a collection of instruments which usually includes drums, tambourines, cymbals, bells, castanets. A gong or very large cymbal or a pair of indian bells is a useful addition, so that there is an instrument capable of making a sustained sound.

The diagrams shown on pp. 71—4 illustrate the kind of preparation which can be useful for presenting each of the effort actions. The mode of presentation is as follows:

Properties of the main effort action	Words which conjure the main effort action
(of the compensatory effort)	(the compensatory effort)
MAIN EFFORT ACTION (compensatory effort)	
Bodily performance associated with the main effort action	Percussion instruments associated with the main effort action
(with compensatory effort)	(with compensatory effort)

There are many methods of presenting effort to young children but, in principle, the way of improving the movement must have some system of working through each of the three properties of an effort action, its weight, space and time components. The children can start off by responding to the words which are in the top right-hand corner of the diagrams. Each of the three properties in the top left-hand corner can be mentioned and worked on in turn, and particular ways of performing the action, which are in the bottom left-hand corner, can be brought in. An example of this method for thrusting might be:

"Dance with vigorous movement on the spot with stamps and jumps; as you jump make your knees thrust strongly up into the air (strong); stand still and take three big breaths (floating compensation); make each jump and stamping movement sharp and pointed (direct); each new movement is going to be so quick that it gives you a surprise (sudden); listen to the melody I am singing and show me by your movements that you can hear it (floating compensation); put your hands to your temples and feel your pulse throbbing, start stamping your feet in time to your pulse; take your hands away and move your shoulders sharply in the rhythm of your pulse; now move your whole body in time with it making each movement with gusto (thrusting); show me by your movement that you remember the tune I sang to you a little while ago (floating compensation); in partners, show your partner clearly the rhythm of your pulse; make a dance together which has in it thrusting movements to the rhythm of your pulse and soft movements like the ones you did to my singing (phrases of thrusting with floating compensation); make clear the softness of the singing part and the toughness of the throbbing part (light and strong)".

Much more help would be given in between each of these suggestions, but this cannot be set out here as it would depend entirely on the class situation. The age of the group would also change the suggestions, but the principles of gradually working on each property of the effort action in strong, direct, sudden

(light, flexible, sustained)

vigorous, with gusto, pierce, spurt, impact, punch, lunge, throb, jolt, tough, marcato

(weightless, undulating)

THRUST
(float)

stamping, jumping, positions, clapping, heartbeat

(breathing)

drum, tambourine

(indian bells, singing)

---

light, flexible, sustained

(strong, direct, sudden)

stir, gentle, undulating, thistle-down, buoyant, vaporous, hover, roundabout, caressing, soft, legato

(vigorous)

FLOAT
(thrust)

gesturing, gathering, on the toes, wrist, chest

(stamping)

indian bells, singing

(drum)

strong, flexible, sudden

(light, direct, sustained)

hitting, whipping, beating, swiping, throwing, flinging, splash, sprawl, rip

(smooth)

> **SLASH**
> (glide)

jumping turns, scattering, twisting, shoulders

(balancing)

cymbals, tambourine

(silence)

---

light, direct, sustained

(strong, flexible, sudden)

smooth, calm, lullaby, soothing, stroking, passing over, straight, legato, lingering

(whipping)

> **GLIDE**
> (slash)

pathways, sole of the foot, palms, linear, gestures

(turning jumps)

silence, continuous roll on cymbal or drum, indian bells

(clashing cymbals)

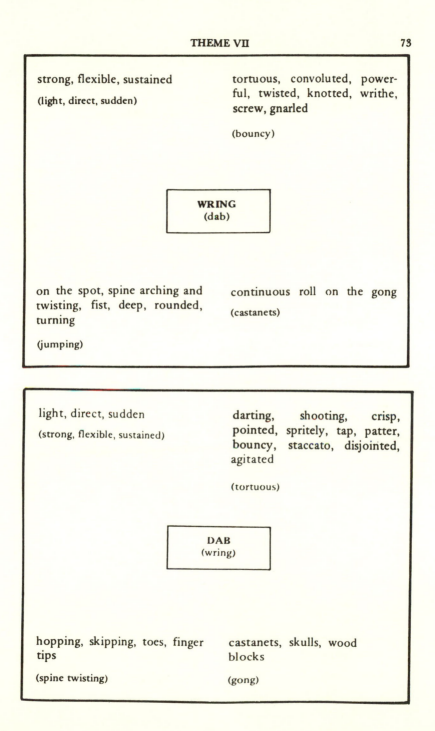

strong, flexible, sustained

(light, direct, sudden)

tortuous, convoluted, power-ful, twisted, knotted, writhe, screw, gnarled

(bouncy)

WRING
(dab)

on the spot, spine arching and twisting, fist, deep, rounded, turning

(jumping)

continuous roll on the gong

(castanets)

light, direct, sudden

(strong, flexible, sustained)

darting, shooting, crisp, pointed, spritely, tap, patter, bouncy, staccato, disjointed, agitated

(tortuous)

DAB
(wring)

hopping, skipping, toes, finger tips

(spine twisting)

castanets, skulls, wood blocks

(gong)

strong, direct, sustained

(light, flexible, sudden)

firm, sturdy, pulling, squeezing, massive, powerful, ponderous, deliberate

(frisky)

PRESS
(flick)

muscular tension, palms, into the floor

(elevated)

continuous roll on the drum or gong

(bells)

---

light, flexible, sudden

(strong, direct, sustained)

flickering, quivery, sparkling, crisp, flutter, whisking, fits and starts, twitch, rippling, frisky

(sturdy)

FLICK
(press)

jumping, turning, leaps, little fingers, leg gestures

(muscular tension)

bells, tambourine

(drum roll)

turn, with compensation in between, building up to some satisfying whole, such as a very brief partner exchange, would remain constant.

The starting-off point could be one of the properties of the action, the other two being gradually brought in. For example: main action wringing, compensation dabbing; start with all manner of twisting movement (flexible), in the spine, the neck, the legs and the wrists; gradually bring in firmness and then sustainment using words like powerful, strong, gradual, slow motion, and helping the mood by accompanying with a gong roll; in between allow the children to hop and jump and shake themselves (dabbing).

Percussive rhythms are a good stimulus for effort actions which can then be worked on as suggested above. For example: main action flicking, compensatory effort pressing: hold a drum by the rim and in the same hand, a bell on a handle. Play a rhythm on the bell: a short shake—short shake—long shake—repeated three times followed by an increasingly loud drum roll. The effort actions made in response to the sound will be flick, flick, flickering; flick, flick, flickering; flick, flick, flickering; pressure. This could be developed into a short dance in twos using partner themes from Theme V, in the form of question and answer or meeting, parting and going round. Spatial ideas from Theme III could also be used in the form of level changes or the size of the movements. Each pair could make the movements in unison, opposition, or with one person as the flicker and the other as the presser. The teacher can work on each of the properties of the effort action while the pair make their own version of the dance.

The percussion instruments can be played by the children while they are dancing so that a group with bells may make a flicking dance, one with drums a thrusting dance, another with cymbals a slashing dance. After a while the group may move on to another instrument and it can be so arranged that the next instrument is one which will stimulate the opposite effort action. The instruments are capable of stimulating far more than one quality; for example, a drum can be beaten loudly for thrusting, tapped on the rim for dabbing and smoothed over with the palm for gliding, the shape of it can be used to illustrate round movements; it can be beaten by different parts of the body or held in the hand while moving in silence. When the teacher's aim is to limit the movement fantasy and use the sound as an aid to effort experience, it is important that the children realise the limitation and concentrate on the one particular way in which the instrument is to be played, i.e. to convey the chosen effort. When percussion is used in this way it is not a stimulus to which a free response is asked but rather an accompaniment to effort actions, the movement being more important than the sound. At another time the sound created can be of more importance than the effort content of the movement, in which case the aim of the lesson will be quite different and would not necessarily come under the heading of Theme VII.

6. TEACHING EFFORT FOR OLDER CHILDREN AND ADOLESCENTS

Whatever ages the pupils are, dynamic changes will be clarified and enriched when they are looked at from the three components of weight, space and time. However, the context in which this will occur is quite different. It would clearly be inappropriate to ask adolescent girls or boys to "dance with vigorous movement on the spot with stamps and jumps"! They would find it hilariously funny, or downright ridiculous.

Certain guidelines can be given. Dancing must be set in motion first by the methods usually adopted, such as sequences taught and remembered, music brought and used as a background, technical difficulties practised or a "piece" worked on by pupils and teachers together for an evening's dance recital or an arts festival. Study of the adverbial qualities is applied then in this dancing context.

The limit of one pair of efforts was suggested for the younger pupils. Here it is inappropriate, opposites being too blatant for the older age group. Similarities may be shown between two qualities nearly alike, such as floating and flicking; or floating and wringing; or floating and gliding. The older pupil is able to perceive these samenesses and to choose the subtle expression she or he wants for the moment in the dance in question.

The technical names for the effort actions can be quite out of place in dance. They are not objectionable for youngsters, but older pupils will have a more developed sense of language, and of the appropriateness of words to different context. These words are the best that could be found. They were in any case a translation from the original German and intended to be appropriate to movement in industry as well as dance in schools. The most helpful attitude to the words is to recognise their inadequacy and provide a mass of other words which can be used in their place according to context. The lists in the right-hand top corners of the boxes on the previous pages give a start. Verbs, adjectives and adverbs can all help. Here are a few verbs:

Consolidate, crystallise, compress, squeeze, expand, dilate, harden, startle, swerve, accent, stress, tense, weaken, droop, stiffen, soften, shiver, burst, fly, give way, crack, disintegrate, grind, crush, liquefy, flow, melt, dissolve, plunge, hasten, sprint, scurry, run, shoot, rush, dart, quicken, force, lag, drawl, linger, plod, trail, slouch, shuffle, limp, shamble, stagger, mince, march, retard, check, curb, slacken, point, steer, deviate, avoid, swerve, sidle, straggle, digress, meander, drift, encompass, caress, etc., etc. Any word book will provide all that is needed.

7. EFFORT ACTIONS AND THE BODY

In the movements used in ordinary day to day activities, in doing things and behaving, efforts occur in a continuous changing rhythm. While doing this, the body is used in continuously changing ways. Joints, surfaces, areas, small muscle groups, isolated body parts, the whole body, move one after the other in an ever changing sequence. A relationship exists between the parts used and the efforts made. While theoretically it would be possible to float, for example, with the palms leading, in fact this is not done. Palms lead into emphatic strong movement; the backs of the hands lead light movements, especially floating.

There is a tendency to allow the natural affinity between body part and effort, apparent in day to day movement, to continue in dance. Strong movements are encouraged in the legs, light ones in the arms, strong from the pelvis, light from the chest. This retention of the everyday inhibits the progression from movement to dance. Adventurous use of the body is to be encouraged so that effort actions and dynamic rhythms occur in likely and unlikely places. Pressing up with back of the hands is less usual than pressing down with the palms. As such it is far more arresting to do and to see. Floating with the arms held out lightly, allowing them to undulate, is more everyday than floating with the arms held into the body, in a sitting position. The latter is interesting, the former boring. A slashing turning jump is "child's play", while a slashing roll into a balance on one hip is exciting.

Just as the body and effort have everyday affinities, so too do actions and efforts. Turning is linked with the flexible efforts, transferring weight with strong ones, gesturing with light ones, jumping with quick efforts, travelling with gliding, etc. Again, retention of this affinity limits the transference from movement to dance. Turns may be strong, gestures direct, travelling slow, transferences sparkling, falling light, extending heavy, etc.

Chasing after novelty through making efforts with unusual body parts and unusual actions is not an end in itself to be pursued. Obviously not. But creative work must entail exploring these possibilities from time to time, in order to provide new expressions, new methods, new styles of dancing, and to include disturbing expressions in the repertoire.

8. EFFORT ANALYSIS

Looking at each other's dance phrases and analysing them in effort terms is enjoyable and another way of coming to terms with quality. Phrases from technique sessions, from improvisation, from learned dances, from folk dance, from films of well-known works and from social dancing can all be used.

The method is simple but has a few pitfalls that a teacher would do well to note:

(a) remember that dance will contain complete efforts, single effort elements, and effort elements in pairs (*see* Themes II and IV).

(b) it will contain a whole mass of quality which, at this stage, youngsters will not be able to discern.

(c) look for obvious movements to analyse.

(d) do not hope to or try to analyse each and all movements.

(e) look for the placement in the body of the effort.

(f) the search for effort in dance is similar to the search for colour in paintings. At this stage, the children will see red, yellow, blue, white, black, orange, etc., but the in-between colours will be ignored. In their dance, they will recognise floating, thrusting, sudden, flexible, etc., but not the in-between qualities.

CHAPTER 8

Theme VIII:Occupational Rhythms

The purpose of this Theme is to link dance with working movement by showing that the same principles are involved in practical and in expressive movement; also to use the rhythms of occupational movement as a stimulus to dance. This is a traditional idea, as there have been work dances since dance began, and many present-day folk dances have this basis. The Theme corresponds musically with learning to compose from work songs and from the sounds created by work. It serves to link Themes VI and VII, and often Theme V also, as the satisfactory use of the body in varied qualities, plus co-operation with others, form the root of working movement. It also serves as a preparation for quality changes, which are dealt with in Theme X.

1. MIMING WORKING ACTIONS

Simple repetitive actions are the best to mime when starting, such as hammering, sawing, pounding. To clarify the action, the following points could be raised:

(a) the shape of the hand so that it shows clearly how the object is held, the shape of the object and its size;
(b) the rhythm that evolves from repeating the action;
(c) the weight and time and space qualities of the action;
(d) the quality of the transition between each action;
(e) how much of the body is involved in the action.

Longer phrases can be mimed involving a whole sequence

of events, such as washing up, laying the table, cutting out
a dress pattern, driving a car; imitating all kinds of work-
men, such as a tailor, a watchmaker, a road mender, a
builder, a typist. Here again the qualities of the actions can be
recognised and made clear. As an example, a builder might
carry a load of bricks on his shoulder, when his action will
be strong and will involve his whole body; he could put
the load down, when the movement will be flexible, slow
and strong as he hoists it off his shoulder; it will be bound
flow and strong and direct as he carefully puts them down;
it will be direct and bound when he puts one brick on top of
another to fit exactly. All sorts of controlled effort will have
been used, most often strong and firm and slow, and
involving a large part of the body.

A typist will use quite different qualities, mainly dabbing
with fingers, small precise movements. A tailor uses a variety
of qualities, large smoothing actions as he spreads out the
cloth, small careful direct and flexible movements as he cuts
out the pattern, going round the corners and changing
direction, small hand movements as he stitches the pieces
together. Doing the weekly wash gives much scope for
variety: rubbing clean, wringing out, the flicking and slashing
as the clothes are shaken out, the smaller movements of the
hand and stretch of the body and arm as the clothes are
shaken out, the smaller movements of the hand and stretch
of the body and arm as the clothes are put on the line, the
slower ironing movements using pressing and gliding.
Children enjoy miming these actions and showing one
another and deciding what qualities are used.

2. WORK IN PAIRS OR GROUPS

Such actions as using a double saw, lifting something heavy,
pulling or pushing a heavy object along, folding the sheets,
making a bed, are great fun to do in pairs. Actions can be
done by a whole group, such as building a house together,
working on a conveyor belt, pulling in fishing nets. Sport
can also be made a theme; a cricket match, tennis, or playing
catch. The following points could be raised to clarify the
action.

(a) Have you both got the same size of object?

(b) Can you make your rhythm fit in with your partner's?

(c) Are you getting in the way of your co-workers?

(d) Can you make your movements fit in with theirs in time and in space?

3. THE RHYTHM OF ACTION

Detail in the movement can be found by looking more deeply into the rhythm. A simple action sequence has a three-part rhythm — the preparation, the action and the recovery. For example, in hammering, the preparation is lifting slowly and lightly (gliding or floating), the action is downwards strongly, suddenly and directly (thrusting), and the recovery is a rebound, light, sudden and direct (dabbing). Each part of the action may have more than one effort quality and consist of several lesser actions; for example, lifting a cup to another place: the preparation is the approach and the grasp, the main action is carrying, and the recovery is setting down and releasing the cup. In a repeated action the rhythm may be: preparation-action-recovery, action-recovery, action-recovery, but the principle of three parts is always there. This detailed view of working actions is not for the young child but is of interest to older people and brings about an awareness of effort rhythms which can later be used in dance.

It is interesting to compare two people miming the same action sequence. The effort rhythms will not be identical, but will be coloured by personal effort preferences and habits. Children are quick to see these and this is one way of awakening interest in their own movement habits, as these are more easily recognised in mime than in dance, to begin with.

4. MOODS AND WORKING ACTIONS

Actions can be performed in a leisurely or hurried way, when the time element of the movement will alter somewhat. The sequence may be started in a leisurely way, become hurried after several repetitions, and then become slower and slower until it tails off. The action may be done haphazardly or precisely; in the former case all the effort qualities will become blurred, while in the latter each one will be more clearly pronounced. A whole range of moods or attitudes towards working actions can be explored, and with it the resulting change in dynamics and speed of the action. It will be found that some attitudes are more suited to one action than another, for example, a very lively mood would not be suitable for a precise job such as embroidery, but it would be suitable for large chopping actions. A leisurely attitude would not be suitable for a job which requires complex timing with a partner, such as tree-felling with partners alternately cutting the trunk, but it would be suitable to the job of rocking the baby's cradle.

Much enjoyment can be gained by trying these things out and watching one another, by working in groups with different or similar moods and seeing what results.

5. TRANSLATING WORK INTO DANCE

Primitives, so-called, did much of their work in a dance-like way, often accompanied by work songs to help the rhythm. This is still done and can be seen in many parts of the world and indeed in Europe. From this come the work dances which form a large part of the folk-dance heritage of many nations. These arise from the kind of working actions with which the people are involved during their daily lives, enhanced by a development of rhythm and pattern inherent in the actions. One example is the treading of grapes in vine-growing areas. To begin with the action is just treading on the spot, then going from one spot to another, then getting a rhythm in the treading steps and then a step pattern, until finally a rhythmical step pattern is evolved which fits in with other people doing the same job. In this way the dance is gradually built up.

(a) Enhancing the rhythm
To translate a working action into dance, the rhythm must be found by repetition until some division in the duration emerges. It is unlikely that a simple duple or triple time diversion will emerge, but it could. More likely, uneven

divisions will be discerned. They can be quantified by finding a common time unit so that, say, durations of 3, 2, 3, 1, 7, 7 emerge. The important point is to find the rhythm which is inherent in the action and not to force the action into a convenient metre. A common rhythm can often be found which will bind together a group of people doing different actions within the same scene. When the rhythm has been found, more flow will come into the movement and it will already be more dance-like, just as the primitive work dances were. The qualities used to colour the rhythm can be clarified and intensified so that the quicker moments are sharply in focus, the flexible moments are spatially enhanced, the light moments perceived and seen.

(b) Enlarging the pattern

The second aid to translating the action into dance, is to take note of the pattern in space which is made by the movement. As the flow from the rhythm takes over, the pattern can easily become enlarged and made clearer or elaborated. The steps from the stance can become more definite, be enlarged and developed into a dance-like step pattern, which is repeatable. Slight leg gestures will have been indicated in the mime and these can be enlarged and brought into the step pattern. If there was an upward movement in the mime, this might be enhanced by bringing in elevation to stress the upward direction. Small movements of the hands can be enlarged to incorporate the whole arm and upper part of the body, so that the shape of the movement becomes more evident. The original mime may be hardly recognisable as such, but a dance motif will have been established that can be developed into a sequence and this, then, into a complete dance with floor patterns.

(c) The emergence of the dance

The narrative, "I am typing", "I am a builder" is not tenable in dance. For a dance to be made which is worth doing or looking at, the enormous and formidable task of translating the rhythms and patterns of the working action into something else has to be done. This is called "creative aesthetic embodiment". It means finding a form or manner of putting together the movement bits in such a way that they synthesise into something unique which contains what the dance artist feels and thinks and discovers about his theme and his medium.

Theme XVI is where this very taxing business is concentrated but beginnings towards it could be included in this Theme.

The first step is to recognise that each movement unit can be treated like a building brick. It must be looked at as something independent which can be dealt with as an object. This is easier to do if the creator is not also the dancer. The units can be placed in time and space wherever and however the choreographer decides. A space, given a front, back, and sides is desirable, like the frame for a picture. The dance units can be performed anywhere in that space, and the discovery that the same movement unit looks different according to its placement is an exciting one. The same unit seen in different places can be achieved by several dancers placed, simultaneously, in parts of the space. Alternatively, one dancer, by repeating the unit, can present it in different parts of the space. This kind of unit construction is the bone structure of composition, and in order for it to live as a unique piece a personal dimension of the artist is needed, a point of view, a comment, a new look at the theme.

The three words, "feel", "think", and "discover", are starting avenues for the choreographer to pursue. What does he feel about the theme? "Feelings" may be sensings from the feeling systems, like seeing, hearing, muscular feeling, or "feelings" may mean private emotive feelings. Both are avenues to pursue in relation to occupational themes. Thinking means in this case allowing thoughts on the theme to flow freely, making connections with other things seen, thought, heard, moved. Logical transformations of the units can be thought about, time schemes be worked out, floor patterns drawn. Discovering involves trying out ideas in the art medium, in this case the movements in the body. One action may lead into another, one juxtapositioning prove abortive, another enlightening.

Discovering what effect lighting has, costume has, speeding up has, doing it all backwards has, is what creative endeavour is all about. Imaginative discovery is said to be putting together of things hitherto apart. The choreographer needs to try to do just that in order to made "a work dance".

6. TASK SUGGESTIONS

(a) Mime the actions of someone who works on the land, or who works in an office. Clarify this by referring to the points under 1 of this Theme.

(b) Choose one part of a mime and repeat it until the rhythm becomes clear. Sing the rhythm as you move.

(c) Accompany on a percussion instrument the rhythm produced by the mime of your partner.

(d) Work in threes and mime the actions of a conveyor belt sequence with three workers, so that the actions of each person link with the other two.

(e) You are planting seedlings in a row. Create a movement motif which can express this and which develops a floor pattern.

(f) Find a second motif which goes well with the "seedling" motif in space and rhythm, and use it to make a two-part motif.

(g) Translate and transform the two-part motif of *(f)* so that it can be presented in a given space to a group of watchers.

(h) You are three burglars surreptitiously entering a house. Mime the actions and show the mood of the burglars.

(i) Learn a folk dance which has a work theme and see how the work movements have been treated.

CHAPTER 9

Theme IX: Shape in Movement

The ideas in this Theme are a progression on the initial spatial ideas in Theme III, and lead towards formed dance.

Shapes in the body are kinesthetically perceived. The articular system, particularly, brings about awareness of the shapes made by the body through skeletal displacement in space, and the muscular system gives awareness of the tensions and forces needed to maintain the shape. The eyes bring messages but are inadequate alone, for their visual field is limited compared to the range of the kinesphere. Hence, patterns and shapes seen or imagined must be transformed into movements guided and controlled by the kinesthetic network.

1. BASIC SPACE PATTERNS

Movements make either *straight* or *rounded* patterns.

(a) Straight lines can be drawn from one place to another anywhere in the kinesphere. Drawing the number "1", or the capital letters I X E T, etc., helps to establish a feeling for these straight pathways. It is easier to lead the movement with the hands and arms and to place the shapes in front of the body or on the floor at first, but they can soon be drawn above or at the side, using spatial areas already experienced in Theme III. When two straight lines are performed consecutively, an *angular* pattern is formed (7 V L W N M and Z). It is important that an appropriate rhythm is used to help in the experience of an angle as one movement, and

not as two straight lines. In the angle the focal point is the spot where the direction changes. This is emphasised by making the first part as an up-beat or preparation, for the second part which takes the main stress, or vice versa.

(b) Rounded movements are smooth. There are no corners or sharp edges, but one continuous line. Drawing the letters C O and numbers 3 6 9 helps to establish this basic pattern and its variants in the body. From rounded movements are derived simple curves (C), circles (O), spirals (6) and repeated curves (3). They can be placed anywhere around the body, be repeated on the other side, performed by both arms simultaneously or consecutively, with any parts of the body, with rising and falling or be turned upside down. Curves can be made while turning, with jumping, with travelling, or while lying down.

(c) Twisted patterns are rounded movements which change direction in the middle. Drawing the letter S and figures 2 and 8 helps to establish this basic pattern in the body. Simple twists (S), repeating twists (8) and twists with spiral (2) appear in letters and numbers, but any variations can be made.

Movement becomes varied when combinations of the four basic space patterns, straight, angular, rounded and twisted, are built up into dance phrases. A natural rhythm will evolve which should be brought out to enhance the composition.

Dance phrases learnt, or fragments from dance pieces, will be full of patterns. Awareness of these will help the young dancers to have that sought-after fusion of action with sensation, movement with meaning. Consciousness of the shapes made in simple technical work helps to bring it alive and make it purposeful and helps the dancer to approach the threshold of aesthetic experience.

2. SPATIAL PROGRESSION AND SPATIAL TENSION

In Theme III the body zones were explained and these combine naturally with the making of shapes. The arms will use the air and upper areas with most ease, but can also go into the leg zone. The legs will more easily stay low in their own zone and will find the floor a good place for pattern making.

All kinds of steps and leaps can be used to create a floor pattern. Circles, figure of eights, zigzags, straight lines, spirals can all be stepped out or danced with jumps and turns.

A pattern in the air or on the floor exists as a spatial concept, which is performed by the body. A body part starts at one end and progresses along the imagined pattern. This is called spatial progression. It takes place in the air or on the floor and is transient in nature. Spatial progressions are easy to imagine but not always easy to appreciate in another, for one may well see the changing body positions rather than the pattern, which emerges "in time", not instantaneously and all at once.

Lines and patterns may also be used in dance as imagined tensions between two body parts or two people. The parts pull away from each other creating a visible relationship or they compress together. A curving arm may be part of an imagined circle; the part not in the body is visibly imagined. These imagined lines or shapes are called *spatial tensions.*

Progressions and tensions mix and merge in dance, but the young dancer should learn to distinguish the one from the other.

There are independent air patterns, independent floor patterns, floor patterns accompanying air patterns, and air patterns accompanying floor patterns.

3. THE SIZE OF MOVEMENT

Movements can be *large* or *small*. There are many stages in between which are passed through in the process of growing and shrinking which is used so often in early dance. The size of movement can be experienced best in relation to shapes and patterns. A rounded pattern can start in the hand, quite small, gradually increasing until the whole body is used, a floor pattern or jumps helping to achieve the final large shape. A twist becomes more coloured when part of it is small and part large. Angular shapes can have one side longer than the other and a spiral results when a circle increases or decreases its size during the movement.

Different parts of the body and variety of size can be seen in dance phrases from established repertoire. The dancer is introduced to new expressions by appreciating size in pieces and is educated and disciplined to master his own body by striving to achieve this spatial aim.

4. BODY SHAPE AND SPATIAL MASS

Achievement of shape in the body is a fundamental goal towards which dancers work. It is called "line" in the body. What are needed are accurate messages from the body telling the dancer whether his or her body is, in fact, taking up the shape or line that he imagines, or not.

The imagined shape is not progressed along, as before, but is replaced by the body's mass. The pattern and the body become one. The term, from sculpture (Rogers L. R.), used for this treatment of the shape is *spatial mass*. The mass, which in the case of dance, is the dancer's body, embodies the shape or line or pattern or series of parallel lines. The shape/line may be large and done by the whole body, or may be small/short and done by smaller parts, a lower arm, a hand, the head, the trunk. The shape/line can remain stationary or can move, retaining its spatial mass character.

The first body shape is taken from the upright standing position. It is called *pin-like* or elongated. From head to toes one line is achieved. This is not difficult in the vertical position, but as soon as the body is tipped into the horizontal or midway between the two, it is another matter. The visual messages lining up the head and trunk with the room walls are gone, the pull of gravity is no longer directly through the trunk into the feet. Even in partial relaxation the body can remain in a "pin" shape vertically. Tipped, the awareness of line through the hips and up the spine is entirely articular and muscular. Much strength is needed. The concept "a line from head to foot" is translated into sensation and intention and the act of lengthening the back and hip line. The line from knees to head is a variant, best learnt first in kneeling then in kneeling and bearing backwards. Linear and horizontal forward, linear and horizontal sideways are both necessary placements of line in the body to be acquired.

The line develops into the cross which is again a basic body shape to be acquired. The line is from head to toe and the line across from hand through shoulders to hand. Again, in the vertical state this is not difficult, but to maintain this shape while tilting the trunk requires much control, sense of line, and strength.

Pin-like is a shape which young children can play with, lying down, on their sides, standing up, growing into a pin-shape, or shrinking from it. But ultimately the technique to achieve it in all situations, and thence to have the freedom to move at will with them, is the aim.

Methods of getting into and out of pin-shapes is fun to discover. Via growing and shrinking, via curved air patterns, via closing-in gestures are examples.

The character of a pin-shape is that it penetrates the space. Knowing this gives some meaning to the movement and some sensations to accompany the action.

The second body shape is *wall-like* or *spread out*. This is also derived from the elementary "large" shape, but it is flat like a sheet of paper and is two-dimensional. It is commonly seen in cartwheels and star jumps. It has variations when the assumed shape is a Y, T, F or K. It can appear horizontally or vertically in the air, during jumps or on the floor, but it always means that the limbs extend away from one another in two dimensions, with the centre of the body as the hub of the shape.

Dancers strive for a wide wall-like position. A really large angle between the outstretched legs, wider than the ordinary person can achieve, is the dancer's aim. It gives an unusualness to the movement, a breadth and virtuosic look. For lesser mortals a strong body with legs straight and stretched in an X shape is aesthetically very pleasing, both to do and to use and to see.

Symmetric, straight or rounded movements can precede a spread body shape, but many other spatial and effort actions can also do so. The character of the shape is that of dividing the space.

The body can be *ball-like* or *rounded*. This is a variant of the elementary "small" body shape. It is commonly seen in somersaults, curling up and back bends. It means that the whole body, and in particular the spine, rounds itself and that instead of the extremities pulling against one another they try to meet and merge. The most usual ball position is curled up over the front, the head linked with the knees and the arms either tucked inside or forming another round shape from the shoulder through the finger tips to the knees. A ball shape can also be made over the back, where the finger tips, head and toes try to meet, or over the sides. The ball can be large or small, but even when a complete round is not made, the relationship between the extremities is always one of trying to meet. The character of this shape is that of surrounding the space in concave positions or displacing it in convex positions.

The body can be *screw-like* or *twisted*. This is a mixture of the elementary "large" and "small" body shapes. The extremities of the body pull against one another, not along an axis, but in different directions around an axis. The lower half pulls clockwise and the upper half anti-clockwise, or vice versa. The resulting twist in the body may be expressed by the limbs in a curled or stretched way, but they are continually twisting away from one another. Two counteracting rounded movements often result in a screw-like body shape.

Shaped arms, independently held, need controlled shape. Rounded arms, together or alone, are needed. Fifth en bas, fifth en avant and fifth en haut are common positions from ballet needed in many styles. The gently rounded state must be learnt by practice. Rounded arms out to the side, rounding upwards by out-turning or downwards by inturning, all manner of circular shapes, can all be seen in dance phrases and practised in dance training, discovered in dance exploration and used in dance composition.

The ability to make parallel arm and leg lines is an essential skill for dancers quite soon in their audience-geared work. It can be included in studies to encourage the co-ordination and build the strength.

Sometimes the body shape is held during a movement, as in rolling, when either a pin or ball-like tension can be kept, or in a cartwheel when the wall-like shape is held. At other times the body shape is a momentary achievement, to be seen or felt and lost. In dance dramas, one kind of body shape may be used as the main carriage of a character, variations of the movement being used within this framework.

5. TASK SUGGESTIONS

(a) Create a sequence containing the contrast between curved and angular patterns in the air.

(b) Write your name in the air, leading with the right, left or both sides of the body. Choose two contrasting letters in it and experiment with where you can place them around you.

(c) Translate in whole body shape a hand movement given by the teacher, which contains rounded, elongated and spread shapes.

(d) Draw a pattern with your finger on the floor. Walk, run, or skip this pattern so clearly that a partner can repeat it.

(e) Master a study given by the teacher on increase and decrease in size of straight lines and circles. Decide how to perform it in threes so that you meet and part during the study. Arrange this dance with an audience in mind.

(f) Translate the words "knobbly", "spiky" and "flat" into body shapes. Use these movement units for an audience-geared composition for two dancers.

(g) Practice, again and again, a sequence on elongated body line given by the teacher.

(h) Watch T.V., especially cartoons, and see how body shape is used to express character.

CHAPTER 10

Theme X: Dynamic Rhythms and Effort Transitions

This Theme is a development of Theme VII, being concerned with the rhythm and dynamics of dancing. Its aim is to experience, recognise and master change from one quality to another. Just as a child uses basic colours in his first attempts at painting and later learns to appreciate shades of those colours and how to merge from one colour into the next, so the dancer progresses from perceiving and performing basic efforts into perceiving transitions from one effort to another.

In Themes II and IV, each effort quality has been recognised separately, making, so to speak, monosyllabic effort-words embedded in movement sequences. Recognising quality changes within one movement is now introduced, making, so to speak, polysyllabic effort-words. For example, a predominantly slashing turning jump followed by a predominantly flicking jump could now be seen in context; the quality of the preparation, the change of the weight factor, the decreasing flexibility on the landing, and the free flow recovery could all be perceived. In painting, two circles, one red and one white, being placed in the context of a background with edges merging into it, or remaining sharp, would illustrate a similar principle. The task is no longer to experience, recognise and master quick and slow movements, but rather becoming quicker, becoming slower; no longer accented and unaccented, but instead impulsive movement which starts with an accent and dies away into unaccented, or a phrase with accents gradually becoming more marked. Intensity and weakness of an effort element are now included, and transitions.

1. TRANSITIONS FROM ONE BASIC EFFORT TO ANOTHER

There are three kinds of basic effort transition, the gradual change, in which one motion factor only is altered, producing a smooth transition, the less gradual change, in which two motion factors are altered, and the abrupt change, in which all three motion factors are altered, producing a sharp transition to a contrasting effort action.

The following table of effort changes may be helpful:

GRADUAL

	Time Change	Weight Change	Space Change
Float	Flick	Wring	Glide
Thrust	Press	Dab	Slash
Glide	Dab	Press	Float
Slash	Wring	Flick	Thrust
Dab	Glide	Thrust	Flick
Wring	Slash	Float	Press
Flick	Float	Slash	Dab
Press	Thrust	Glide	Wring

LESS GRADUAL

	Weight-Time	Time-Space	Space-Weight
Float	Slash	Dab	Press
Thrust	Glide	Wring	Flick
Glide	Thrust	Flick	Wring
Slash	Float	Press	Dab
Dab	Press	Float	Slash
Wring	Flick	Thrust	Glide
Flick	Wring	Glide	Thrust
Press	Dab	Slash	Float

ABRUPT

Space-weight-time changes or complete contrast:

Float	to	Thrust
Thrust	to	Float
Glide	to	Slash
Slash	to	Glide
Dab	to	Wring
Wring	to	Dab
Flick	to	Press
Press	to	Flick

Gradual transitions occur in movements where there is a smooth change from one quality into another. Only one element changes.

Suppose: "a floating quality is used in gently circling arms, perhaps from second position through fifth en avant to fifth en haut, repeated several times, allowing the wrists to give a little. The last one opens to the second position with the palms upwards, then lifts a tiny bit while twisting inwards with a sudden feeling and speed-up (flick). The hands slow down as they continue up a little (float), and the arms settle in demi-seconde (glide)".

Here is a phrase entirely lightly performed, changing from one basic effort to another by altering the space or the time element.

Suppose: "a sweeping single arm movement, from forward to high to backward to deep, with trunk tilt and twist accompanying, performed vigorously and with central body flow (slash); the arm continues and leads into a forward lunge or tombé, clearly focused, forward and far, performed equally vigorously (thrust)".

The whole action is speedily over, it is an action of two "syllables", strong and speedy throughout, changing from flexible to direct.

Note that when gradual transitions are made the spatial pattern is a continuous one, if the same body part performs the changed effort. Look at the chart which shows the three possible variants for each gradual effort transition.

Less gradual changes involve two element alterations.

Suppose: "a balance or piqué on the right foot, with free leg backwards, performed with sudden lightness, directed (dab), the arms lifting to HL and RF slowly, while balanced (glide); the back leg bends in sharply and strongly, with parallel rotation, while the supporting leg bends or plié equally vigorously (thrust); the free leg gestures, out-turning, through forward to open into a deep step DLF, the body twisting round to the left beyond the step, the arms closing in behind and across, performed slowly and strongly (wring)".

Here a gradual change during the balance (two syllable action) is contrasted with a less gradual change. Another body part (free leg) initiates change when strength and speed are applied, still direct. The wringing twist is done still strongly, but slowly and flexibly. If the transition here is smooth, which it may well be, because the leg is keeping a continuous pattern, then probably "press" is introduced, after the sharp inward gesture to make a "two-syllable" action. But if the wring appears immediately out of the thrust, a sensation of slight abruptness is felt, a definite change, not an appearance of something new, unnoticed.

Two-element changes produce a somewhat abrupt rhythm, sometimes resilient, always new and a little unexpected in phrasing. A gliding, smooth movement will not dissolve, but may explode. A thrust will not be vigorous for long but will be becalmed. A floating arm circle may suddenly whip round, or condense into focused pressure, or suddenly sparkle. Look at the chart which shows the three possible variants for each effort action.

Abrupt changes juxtapose opposites. The rhythms are always interrupted, and because of the total difference in quality they can appear unrestful, incongrous, extraordinary, disconnected, or confusing.

Suppose: "a series of intricately and delicately performed small jumps (flick-dab), interspersed with broad, whole body, languorous but tensed outwards actions (press)".

Or: "Vigorous and virtuoso-type turning jump, perhaps jete en tournant (slash), interrupted out of nothing with smooth, light slow walks (glide)".

Or: "An adagio change from arabesque to attitude (float), interrupted by a wide, athletic split jump (thrust)".

The mind boggles!

Apart from the fact that these changes are extremely difficult to do and would, most likely, have gradual or less gradual transitions inserted for sheer technical reasons, the incongruity shouts. As a means to surprise, to comedy, to sudden drama, to confusion, these effort changes point the way.

In planning a piece in which opposite characterisation is to be included, exemplified by these over-obvious pairs, Beauty and the Beast, the Wicked Fairy and the Innocent Babe, the Priest and the Miserable Sinner, The Rich Man and the Poor Little Orphan, opposite pairs of effort would be excellent starting points. In texture themes, sparkling against grumbling, soft against jagged, enveloping against darting out, opposites would again be a start.

As always in effort work, the dancing must come first and the effort come as a colouring to the form, if dancing rather than movement is being sought. Play which starts from opposite effort actions, or gradual effort transitions, or less gradual changes will stick at movement feeling. Until the dancing action and the movement feeling are one, aesthetic experience has not begun. The merge of technique with feeling has to take place in order to transform self-indulgence and mechanical capering.

2. OTHER TRANSITIONS BETWEEN BASIC EFFORT ACTIONS

Important or imposing movements are probably coloured by effort actions, clarified in space/time/weight use. When a sequence goes from one imposing movement to another, and so on, the transitions just described are occuring. However, dancing includes many less imposing movements, those, as it were, in brackets. They are done but hardly seen. These are transitions with only one clear effort element. They occur very often in repetitions.

Suppose: "Galloping broadly and rhythmically; the outward first step is the important and noticed one, the closing step is simply a transition; the metre is 3/4".

The first step is clear in space (say direct), in time (say slow, speeding up), in weight (say strong). The second is simply quick, neither light nor strong, neither direct nor indirect.

Suppose: "A series of imposing, slow advancing steps; the transference is important, the gesture in between being transitional".

The step is clear in time (sustained), in space (direct), in weight (strong), the gesture is simply light.

Suppose: "An arm gesture, out-turned, starting with the little finger side of the right hand near the left shoulder; with the back of the hand leading throughout, pass through DR, HR, and HL, with pressure. Return to the starting position".

The gesture is strong, directed, and sustained. The transition is simply flexible.

It is also likely that the transition may sometimes simply be freely flowing, not clear in space/time/weight but clear in flow only.

3. FLOW AND EFFORT RHYTHMS

Main movements need not be performed with complete effort clarification in space/time/weight. Indeed in dance they are often not so clarified. In work actions with objects the need to handle the material strongly or lightly, make direct or flexible uses of the available space, and use the available time quickly or slowly, imposes a dynamic with tripartite clarity. In dance, this is not so. The flow element, the extra element concerned with response to information from within and without, is present again and again in dance, permeating the entire body and "muddling" the effort patterns.

Treating dance as an art form, a medium for symbol making, performing, and appreciating, cannot leave effort unaffected. The effort action-rhythms of work and interpersonal communication and of privacy are genuine rhythms connected with and part of the person as a person. The effort rhythms of dance are made to happen. They are intentional and not symptomatic manifestations. They are simulations of feeling, simulations of relationships, simulations of power (*see* Langer S. K. 1953).

Flow appears as a response to input from outside, from memory, and from chemical changes, in its genuine condition. In dance, these responses are simulated. We know what it is to feel adrenalin flow through the body. While this may happen to dancers in class time, it is more likely that it will not. We simulate it. We allow the fluidity and exaggeration, the ebbing and flowing of the movement to happen without the actual chemical cause. This is part of the dancer's skill. We fill our ordinary dance exercises with the kind of fluidity and vibration which would normally be the result of chemistry, but we do it without. We simulate it.

The messages from the dancing body of cutaneous, articular, muscular kinds, arouse sensations of movement which are, to dancers, thrilling. This thrill of dancing, once felt, is the message of the body. Response to it produces flow quality. We respond to our movements. The fluidity increases, the restraint is sensitive, the phrasing is outpouring or withheld, tentative or gushing.

All this changes effort actions. Two things can happen:

(*a*) Flow becomes added so that each effort has two different manners of qualifying the movement or moment.

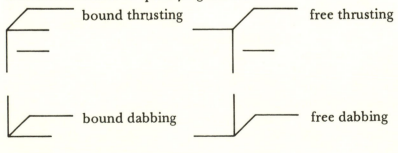

bound thrusting   free thrusting

bound dabbing   free dabbing

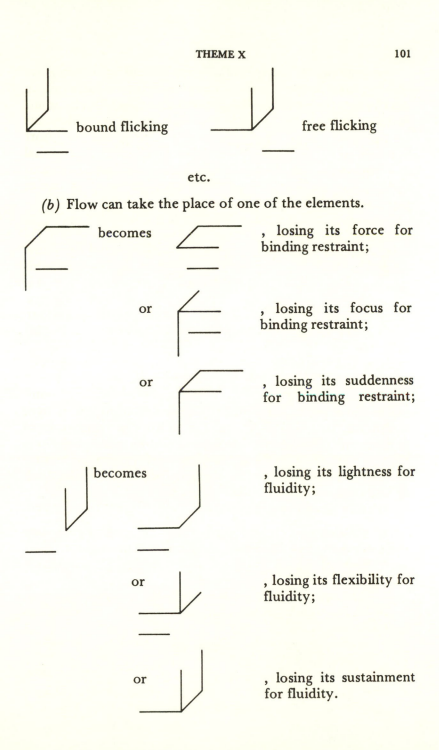

bound flicking   free flicking

etc.

(b) Flow can take the place of one of the elements.

becomes   , losing its force for binding restraint;

or   , losing its focus for binding restraint;

or   , losing its suddenness for binding restraint;

becomes   , losing its lightness for fluidity;

or   , losing its flexibility for fluidity;

or   , losing its sustainment for fluidity.

Variants can be found on the other efforts by allowing free flow to take the place of lightness, flexibility or sustainment, and bound flow to take the place of strength, directness and suddenness.

(c) Flow can take the place of two elements.

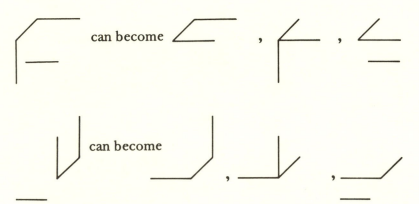

Refer to Chapter IV for other two-element dynamic qualities.

The flow which is so vital to dancing is to be encouraged by the teacher at all times. He will help youngsters to perform with flow, to recognise with and to create with flow. He will link these dynamic rhythms with phrases of actions and sequences, so that the dancing becomes infused with qualities sensed and qualities achieved.

A teacher's aids include:

(a) percussion, tuned and untuned, which provide dynamic changes in their own medium;

(b) pictures which show colour changes, light and shade changes;

(c) sculptures and 3D models which show texture changes;

(d) music which shows sonority changes, instrumental texture changes;

(e) films, videos of interpersonal exchanges, of dances with dynamic breadth;

(f) words, poetry, stories;

(g) a good technique himself to demonstrate dynamic changes, or a first-rate comprehension of effort rhythms with

a wide vocabulary and qualitative prosodic delivery to explain them;

(h) a real interest in and intention to bring about in youngsters the thrill of the sensations and skills of dancing rhythms.

4. PHRASES OF EFFORT

The comprehension of effort phrases, their complexity and variety, is achieved most reliably through notating them. For this, additional markings are used.

Note the following:

(1) A circle over the effort graph diagonal means that the effort is made during stillness. The circle is the Labanotation "pause sign". Here, the starting position is forcefully direct.

(2) A light preparation; note the brackets to indicate the preparatory nature of the lightness, typical of many phrases.

(3), (4) A two-part phrase continues after the preparation, with a flexible and increasingly strong effort dissolving into a very strong, direct and slightly sudden effort. Note the plus and minus signs added to the effort graph to denote, roughly, the amount of a motion factor. Double or treble pluses and minuses may also be used. Note the phrase line written over the two graphs, linking them.

(5) A free flow recovery bracketted, which is also a preparation for the next phrase.

(6) Slightly strong with increasing bound flow begins the phrase; note the crescendo sign used for "increasing".

(7) Very sudden effort, repeated, resulting in vibration. Note the repetition dots before and after the sudden effort.

(8) The phrase ends in stillness, very lightly held and directed with the flow not stopped but still freely streaming.

(9) The final effort is suddenly made with diminishing lightness, approaching a heavy state.

(10) The whole phrase is given double bar lines, as in music and Labanotation, to denote beginning and end.

Note that a basic effort occurs only once in this whole phrase, at (4), and then with clarification of degree on two motion factors.

Phrases such as this are typical of dance movement. Preparation-action-recovery is a constant rhythm, with the action being made up of one, two, three or more parts. Appreciation of technique phrases, phrases in choreographic works, phrases made by students and children are all illuminated by effort analysis. Analysing provides evidence of moments of importance, of lack of clarity, of invention weakness, of style consistency.

Established artists, especially those who create new styles of work, such as Bournonville, Graham and Humphrey, used clusters of effort phrasing habitually which came to be associated with them. The style occurs after lengthy search for something which is fundamentally enlivening to dancing. Graham's "contraction and release" are well known technical terms. They are words for effort clusters. The contraction is sudden and strong, occuring in the centre of the body, and elsewhere. The release retains bound flow as the strength diminishes and the sudden accent dissolves into sustainment.

Humphrey's "suspension, fall, recovery" phrase is also well known, and can be seen as an effort cluster particularly associated with the weight factor. The suspension, upwards, is light or strong, in varying degrees, with sustainment usually but sometimes suddenly accented. The fall gives into gravity, is downward, gives temporary heaviness, through letting go the suspended light or strong quality. The recovery is the recapturing of the weight, in, again, a light or strong quality. The flow, space, and time factors are interspersed upon this fundamental weight rhythm of controlling, giving in, controlling.

Established dance teachers, and dance "schools", use technical terms for dynamics and effort which are not the standard effort vocabulary. They are more evocative of quality and constitute particular clustering, or effort "words" made out of effort element "letters". A good dance teacher will use these terms and find out what they are, precisely, in terms of motion factor rhythms and phrases. In this way effort theory, so useful to dynamic dancing, can easily be related to all kinds of dance style. An easy interchange of words and terms is recommended so that "contraction", for example, does not remain an isolated Graham term, but is seen in the context of effort and dynamics as a whole.

5. DYNAMIC STRUCTURES AND EFFORT COMMITMENT

Dynamics and effort are terms which are not identical in meaning, although they have been used interchangeably in this book, in an attempt to overcome the problem of the undance-like sound of the word "effort". A particular distinction needs to be made to high-light the specific concept of effort phrases from a more general concept which is indicated, here, under the word "dynamics".

Dynamics, in choreography, concerns the interplay of forces between the dancers, their dance, and the audience. A spectator of a dance happening is caused to enter into it dynamically: His eyes move from dancer to dancer, with varieties of speed and intensity, interest and involvement. The choreographer and director cause these reponses through through manipulating dynamic components, movements, use of downstage/upstage, lighting, stillness, pace, personal projection, to name only a few. Fitted into this framework of dynamic forces, is the individual dancer's own performance. Obviously his costume, spatial patterns, stage placement, and so on, influence the content of his role in the dynamic interplay between him and the audience. But, over and above these, he has at his command the whole range of effort possibilities which provide a quite specific dynamic contribution.

Two strands are considered, the *dynamic structures* given to the dance by the choreographer and the *effort commitment* of the dancer as he performs those dynamic structures. The choreographer sets the pace, the rhythms, the durations, the accents, the length of phrases, the climaxes, that is, the

whole dynamic structure of the dance, of each role, and
of each phrase. He may pre-plan it before he meets his
dancers, he can certainly contemplate and manipulate its
parts before and during the whole rehearsal period. The
structural units constitute the "dynamic bricks" in the
building of his piece, to be designed and redesigned until
the dynamic whole he wants is constructed. The dancer
dances these structures. He has to match the demands with
his performance by producing the variety of effort which this
will achieve. He does so by his effort commitment. This is
a mixture of effort technique and personal involvement.
Strength is produced, technically, by muscular control, which
is learnable, and should be capable of being produced, at
will. But this kind of strength is insufficient and unsatis-
factory. A dancer is a person, not a body, and personal
commitment is his artistry. The strength is produced,
effectively, by his personal commitment to the forces in his
body. He has to feel them, control them, project them,
simultaneously, three distinct processes. The four motion
factors all require this treatment in the complex rhythmical
mixtures already described.

The dancer's personal effort commitment contributes to
the dynamic interplay between dancers, dance, and audience
by bringing to life the choreographer's dynamic structures.

It is therefore of paramount importance that dance
technique is seen to be part of this interplay, from the
dynamic stand point. Technique phrases, from simple
beginner level to advanced ballet enchainement or Graham-
based sequences, have dynamic structures. The teacher's
task is to search for them, to find them, to know how to
produce them, and to convey them. He will do this, in part,
by eliciting personal effort commitment from each student.

(For further reading, see North M. 1972, Lamb W. 1956,
Laban R. 1947 and 1960.)

CHAPTER 11

Theme XI:Orientation in Space

This Theme contains a development of the principles given in Theme III and is connected with Theme IX. The objective word for this Theme is *"where"*; into what direction do I move the different parts of my body and how are these directions organised?

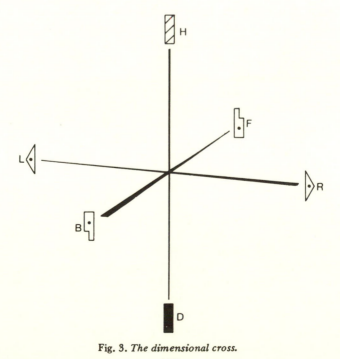

Fig. 3. *The dimensional cross.*

In day-to-day life, the space around us is full of "things", furniture, houses, people, tools, equipment. Our movements are organised by the placement of these "things", and by the way in which we relate to them. In dance, these "things" are not there. The room is empty, the stage is bare, there is simply a void. An articifical scheme is needed to transform space from a void into a framework to which movements can be related and orientated. In theory any scheme could be tried, but one which is related to the proportions of the human body and the dimensions of the world we live in is preferable (*see* Le Corbusier 1954, Critchlow K. 1969 and Ghyka M. C. 1977). The beginning of this scheme is the dimensional cross (*see* Fig. 3; *see also* Laban R. 1966).

1. ESTABLISHING THE DIMENSIONAL CROSS OF REFERENCE

There is an *up-down dimension*. When this direction passes through the body it follows the line of the spine ending exactly between the feet or exactly above the head. The simplest way to feel this is for the hand to progress along the line, accompanying the movement with rising and falling in the rest of the body.

There is a *side-side dimension*. When this direction goes through the body at the waist it extends to right and left into the space. It is connected with the width of the body. This can be felt by starting with both arms at the centre and pulling out to either side simultaneously, feeling width.

There is a *forward-backward dimension,* which can pass through the centre of the body and extends into space in front and behind. This is best felt by starting with one hand at the centre in front of the waist and one behind the waist, and pulling out forwards and backwards simultaneously.

Thus six directions are established, all radiating from a common centre (*see* Fig. 3); upwards, downwards, to the right, to the left, forwards and backwards. Note the symbols used for these directions. In large whole-body actions into these directions, the centre of the cross is conceived as coinciding with the centre of the body. The body can co-ordinate to follow these centrally placed dimensions which can be performed as a continuous progression leading with one side of the body; the resulting actions will be rising, falling, crossing, opening, retreating and advancing. This is called the *dimensional scale* (*see* Fig. 4) and can be performed with alternate sides of the body leading the movement.

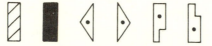

Fig. 4. *The dimensional scale.*

The dimensional cross is a logical form (*see* Lyons J. 1968), or a spatial idea. The dimensional scale is six movements. It is a way of embodying the logical form, which entails decisions on the number of and order of directions, on the body parts to be involved and on the dynamics with which to phrase the whole.

(a) Lines parallel to the cross of reference.
The dimensional cross is placed notionally in the centre of the body. Our limbs may follow it there or may follow parallel to it, placed elsewhere in the kinesphere. A line parallel to the vertical up/down dimension may be imagined at the right side. Or it may be in front of the body. The line(s) are then "embodied" by the dancer by either:
  (i) progression along them;
  (ii) creating spatial tensions along them,
  (iii) performing them in the mass of the body as body shapes and designs (*see* Rogers L. R. 1969).

(b) The dimensions as spatial tensions
Verticality is a fundamental tension. Above and below are the appropriate prepositions. Two parts of the body or two people may create this tension. They may move along the vertical line, towards and away from each other. They may move elsewhere in a parallel relationship, setting up an interest in the vertical tension between the two parties. Horizontality is similarly treated, in both the right/left and the forward/backward dimensions.

Suppose: "Starting low down, crouched, hands together in front of the waist; rising slowly progressing along the vertical line until nearly fully extended throughout the body; at the last moment the knees bend as the arms stretch providing a spatial tension between H and D."

Suppose: "Kneeling; both arms lift sideways, and advance to pause at LF and RF, the back of the hands leading; strength appears as the pause approaches, and suddenly increases in a stop; a spatial tension R − L is set up between the two hands."

(c) The dimensions as spatial mass or body design.
The dancer's body can "be" the up/down dimension. Of course the body is a mass in space all the time, but not consciously so, nor expressively so. In order to make the statement, "my body is vertical", the whole dynamic co-ordination of the body will respond by eliminating excrescent bulges and exaggerating the vertical potential. The arms may be above the head, or perhaps the lower arms be lifted to state "up" from the elbows. A knee may be lifted so that a lower leg can state "down". Horizontality requires similar treatment.

Suppose: "The dancer sits balanced on his seat; the feet are off the floor and the lower legs, together, state "horizontal forwards"; one arm parallels them; the head tilts back to parallel again."

Here is a complex embodiment of horizontality by the body's mass. This is hard to do but interesting to see. It is especially exciting if, say, a spin on the seat can occur while the horizontality is held. It could dissolve into a spatial progression, or finish as a spatial tension.

Choreographers use these ideas again and again. Graham's *Diversion of Angels* has many examples of dimensional movement in the dancer's body mass. Among other directions, horizontality in this work is noticeable; her dancers lie or lean to state "right/left" in their trunks. Parallel leg and arm gestures, horizontal, abound as foils to tilted body designs.

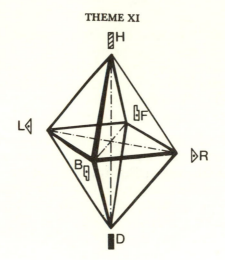

Fig. 5. *The octahedron.*

(d) The octahedron.
The dimensional cross forms the skeleton for an octahedron
(*see* Fig. 5). The poles at each end of the dimensional cross;
high (H), deep (D), right (R), left (L), forward (F) and
backward (B), are linked by peripheral lines, forming a body
with eight triangular-shaped facets. Each pole or apex has
four peripheral lines from it. Hence:

H — F	H — R	and similar from D
H — B	H — L	
R — F	F — H	
R — B	F — R	
R — H	F — L	and similar from L and B
R — D	F — D	

These octahedral lines are embodied either as· spatial
progression, when the imagined lines are progressed along, or
as spatial tension, when a tension between the two ends of
the line is presented, or as spatial mass, when the body parts
become the line.

Suppose: "the arms start in D, move to F, to L and R respectively, and to D again. This is a standard port de bras, fifth en bas, through fifth en avant to second position, and back to fifth en bas. Alternatively, after the progression to L and R the left may go to F and the right to B, both thence to H, and return via L and R to D."

Every dancer has done and seen these patterns; they occur in "class" daily, in modern and classical styles. But the connection with an octahedron may not be conscious. The sequence described, which is spatial progression along the edges of the octahedron, embodied by the arms, can well be accompanied by moves of the rest of the body.

Suppose:

(i) D———►F with knee bends and intention D (plié);

(ii) F———►L and R with return to standing;

(iii) L———► F, R———►B with a step by the right foot F, the left leg extending, but still touching the floor;

(iv) F and B ———►H with turning on the spot, gathering in with the hands;

(v) H———►L, and R———►D, with stillness, on the toes (relevé).

The total body experience and body expression of such a spatial sequence brings about moments of spatial tension and also of spatial mass which are exciting to realise and achieve. The body shape or design arrived at after (i) depends on whether the knees bend forwards or outwards, are done with parallel legs or out-turned legs. The trunk could contract during it or not, producing an alternative body shape. After (ii), the rising up and opening could bring the necessary dynamic to state, "my body is in the shape of a cross". Alternatively a counter-tension could be set up between the arms retreating to the side against a push forward by the chest and face towards F, creating a spatial tension. During (iii), which is a simple arabesque statement, the counter pulls F and B from hand through shoulders to hand, and from D to H from foot through spine to head, producing a lively body design. And so on.

Quite another style of embodiment would be seen, if the

angularity became important. The pointed "roof" of the octahedron, the pointed sides, etc. can be sharply and percussively produced in the body's mass, using kneeling, lying, leaning over, jumping up, with possibly a link with architectural forms.

It need not be said that the octahedron, which is purely a referential framework, should not inhibit movement but provide incentive to new movement. It should also be seen as a way of appreciating shapes and patterns made in class and in choreographies by providing some framework with which they may be seen to conform or conflict.

(*See* 3 *(b)* of this chapter for embodiment checks. p. 127.)

(e) Dimensions of the general space.
The dimensional cross of reference is useful for the body in its kinesphere, through the means already described, and it is useful also for contructive use of the general space.

Imagine the cross of reference in the middle of the room or stage. Its up/down dimension pierces the centre of the ceiling and floor, its side/side dimension pierces the walls, and so does the forward/backward dimension. See how the walls are parallel to its up/down dimension, how the lines joining the walls at the corners reiterate that dimension, how the windows and doors state it, how people standing in the room repeat it. Notice how the right/left dimension is stated by the upper and lower edges of the front and back wall, how the walls at the side are topped and bottomed by lines parallel to the forward/backward dimension. One can imagine an imaginary framework to which movement can relate.

Notice the difference between the dimensional cross of reference of a room and that of the kinesphere of each person in the room (*see* Hutchinson A. 1970 and Preston-Dunlop V. 1969 for "cross of axes" theories in Labanotation). It is easy to see if they face different directions and all make a movement to F. Each person's F is in front of them, to the front of their kinesphere, not to the front of the room. Only when all face front will the F of the individual and the F of the room coincide. Only the up/down dimension is always common to both. Try facing individual fronts and all moving to F of the room. Each person has a different direction according to his own front, but all are parallel.

The dimensions of the room provide a new source of material for pattern making. A fresh embodiment of the dimensional scale can be made. Phrases of movement designed to take the dancer across a R/L room dimension form an excellent problem. Structures are necessary otherwise anything will do. Step patterns and jump patterns can be a helpful start using F, B, R and L directions only. The dancers will find that facing the room front requires a step to the right, open or across, that facing L requires backward steps, that facing R requires forward steps, etc. Choosing the transition from one to the other provides problem solving opportunities. A simple metre to stimulate rhythm is helpful — perhaps a 9/8 at moderate tempo. One solution over a four-bar phrase would be:

    (i)   start facing F, three gallops to the right, the last turning to face L;

   (ii) a step pattern, starting with right foot, forward, back, back, the second "back" becoming a skip turning to the left to face R;

  (iii) three quick steps and a long slow step forward, ending with a brushing gesture through by the left foot, rising on the right, turning to face B;

  (iv) step open left, step open right swinging half round to the right, to face F, step open left;

   (v) repeat.

Movements involving spatial progression such as that just described are simple and straightforward problem-solving exercises. Using gestures, arm movements and trunk tilts requires more ability to compose. Organising the gestures according to the dimensional directions, with parallel body relationships, requires skilful performance as well as compositional imagination. Using spatial tension, octahedral links and spatial mass embodiment requires the beginnings of artistry. Here is work progression.

(f) Spatial duos.

Spatial problems for partners can be put in the following words:

    (i) matching, doing the same;

    (ii) mirroring, a right/left transposition;

    (iii) transposing, forward/backward and up/down transposition;

    (iv) completing, supplying the second half;

    (v) complementing, supplying a congruent pattern which merges/parallels/links;

    (vi) opposing, putting up against down, forward against back;

    (vii) contrasting, putting progression against mass, large against small, curve against angle;

    (viii) in adjoining kinespheres;

    (ix) sharing a kinesphere;

    (x) distanced kinespheres;

    (xi) with supports and lifts.

Recall how a duo (*see* Theme V) can be done for each other or for an audience. With more control of the general space and the kinesphere, the presentation for an audience should be better placed, both in the body and in the space. It should show a grasp of line and shape.

(g) Counter-direction.

Monolinear movements are simple for youngsters. A straightforward statement about one direction is made. After a time these appear and feel obvious, even naïve. "I rise" or "I retreat" does not go very far towards dancing. Many dance movements are polylinear, embracing a three-dimensional use of space. The problem is to control directions while not inhibiting the dance overmuch.

Counter-direction occurs when two opposing directions are used simultaneously, or built up sequentially. Up is used with down, forward with backward, HR with DL. The directions are embodied in limbs and trunk so that opposing spatial tensions are set up. These can be in stillness or moving. They range in difficulty from two hands moving towards each other, palm approaching palm, to a sliding fall

FD with arm, head, trunk pulling BH, with a hand BD forming a second support.

(h) Chordic movement.

Three simultaneous directions form a chord. The chords may first be in any direction, with the co-ordination of three different things being the emphasis. Then orientation of the chords into dimensions may be attempted. This is easy if the directions chosen and the limbs embodying them are compatible, say arm H, arm L, and leg F. It is quite another matter when leg B, L or R, or H is chosen, or arm D. Trunk in any of the horizontal directions or D is taxing. Kneeling and lying may be used. Strength and body flexibility are needed.

These chords are seen in dance pieces again and again. They are lovely to see. Turning while in a chordic situation, or chordic tensions in flight, can be technically brilliant. At any rate, they give aspiring dancers something to aim for.

(i) Regular forms.

A comprehensive group of regular forms in the octahedron, logically based and hierarchically arranged, can be traced. These consist in regular shapes following peripheral and central lines in such a way that balanced circuits appear. This is a major study area which cannot be included in this Theme. Appendix II outlines the main issues (*see* page 201).

2. ESTABLISHING THE DIAGONAL CROSS OF REFERENCE

Directions can follow a diagonal line. There are four such lines and they are:

    (a) high-right-forward (HRF) to deep-left-backward (DLB);
    (b) high-left-forward (HLF) to deep-right-backward (DRB);
    (c) high-left-backward (HLB) to deep-right-forward (DRF);
    (d) high-right-backward (HRB) to deep-left-forward (DLF).

These four lines pass through the centre of tbe cube and extend into space; if one imagines a cube in the centre of the room these diagonal lines will reach towards the eight

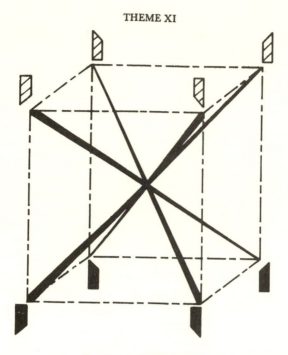

Fig. 6. *The diagonal cross.*

corners of the room (*see* Fig. 6). The centre of the cube may coincide with the centre of the kinesphere and the centre of the body. In this situation the eight diagonal directions can be felt by and performed in the whole body. Any order may be used, but the order above has merit, in that it follows a logical sequence. When the four diagonals are performed fully by the whole body, with the right side leading in the order given above, the resulting sequence is called the *diagonal scale* (Laban R. 1966) (*see* Fig. 7). It will be seen that there is a continuous change between high and deep movements, that there are two forward-backward and two backward-forward movements and that the open-closed series is open-closed, closed-open, closed-open, open-closed.

Fig. 7. *The diagonal scale.*

The legs move congruently as in the dimensional scale, in that all high movements are supported on the toes and all deep ones by lowering the centre of gravity and bending the knees deeply. Kneeling is used in the second and fourth movement, on the right knee. In the second movement the right arm crosses over in front of the body, causing a twist against the kneeling leg. In the fifth movement the arm crosses again in front while the leg crosses behind. The body also arches, bends and twists as in the dimensional scale but, as a diagonal is the integration of three dimensional directions, so the movement of the body is a combination of three actions, rising or lowering, with opening or closing, with advancing or retreating. The spine will not only rise but will arch and bend at the same time, not only lower but round and contract as well. Because of this the diagonal directions are more difficult to master. They are also more mobile and the opposite ends of each diagonal give completely contrasted movements, requiring flexibility and mobility for good performance.

(a) Movement variations on the diagonal.
The same methods can be used to make variations of movement on the diagonal directions as were used with the dimensional cross. The diagonals can be progressed along, in both directions, largely or with small use of distance, with any body parts. Spatial tensions can be set up, using counter-direction. The diagonal can be performed by the body's mass. Superb opportunities exist for extended arabesques into these diagonals, supported on one foot, or in kneeling, or with hand support too.

Parallel body use is again helpful, especially between leg and arm gestures. It is used again and again in choreographies. Look at dancers on film or on T.V. Recognise the tipping of the trunk, the diagonal lines, the parallel limbs. Get used to the unstable look of diagonal moves and contrast them with the stable look of dimensional moves.

Embodying the diagonal requires constraints. The whole point of them as references is that they should clarify actions. The orientation of the trunk especially needs to be looked at so that the 3-dimensionality of diagonals is present.

(i) In HRF and DRF, the part of the trunk leading into the direction is the right front flank, from the collar bone over the breast, from the right front edge of the pelvis into the thigh. The line goes from the top of the head, over the right forehead, down the outside of the eye, over the outside of the cheek-bone and jaw. Enlivening of this line in the body, demand for messages from it of placement, begins to produce orientated diagonal movement. The arm is not difficult; it can be visually in the high or deep diagonal. The supporting leg, the right, may be parallel or out-turned. Parallel gives an excellent feeling for the diagonal at first, but obviously in action out-turned will also be used. The left leg and arm will be parallel, related as decided, but linking with the right arm. The shoulder girdle may twist to the left a little. If it does, there should be a conscious decision to do so, not a "maybe", "perhaps". The method of getting into and out of this situation is again to be decided. Possibly progression from DLB in a closed position, i.e. from a central contracted ball in spatial counter-tension, or from upright body mass, tilting over into the diagonal. The important point is that orientation means knowing where each part is in space and practising this until it is achieved, and describing it until it is understood, and looking for it until it is recognised.

(ii) In HRB and DRB the diagonal flank is from the top of the head, behind the ear, over the shoulder blade, down the right back ribs to the buttock. This provides backward diagonal orientation. Arm and leg behaviour is congruent.

(iii) In HLF, etc., orientation to all the left diagonals is a simple right/left transposition of those on the right, but the limbs may cross over in step and gesture.

In addition to basic orientation, the trunk may also contract over each surface or elongate and arch over them. The supports for high diagonals may be on the toes, for deep diagonals with deep knee bends or kneeling. Each teacher must decide what he wants. Legs may support or gesture, arms may reach out, the trunk may tilt. Jumps and falls may be used but the basic orientation remains.

(b) The cube.

When the eight diagonal directions are linked together

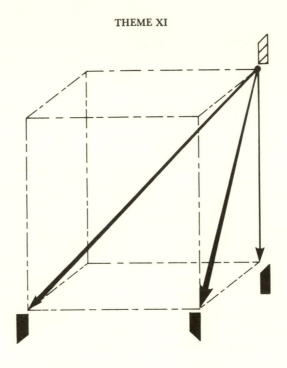

Fig. 8. *Central, over edge and over plane links.*

peripherally it will be found that the cube is made. The cube
has six facets which provide the roof, the floor, and the four
walls of the kinesphere. The feeling of the dancer when
orientated within a referential cube is of a solid body on a
firm base with shooting diagonals. The peripheral links of the
cube provide a reference for extremely mobile sequences
with much turning and twisting. There are two kinds, *over
edge* and *over plane*. High-right-forward to deep-right-forward
is an example of over edge; high-right-forward to deep-right-
backwards is an example of over plane; high-right-forward
to deep-left-backwards is an example of a central link (*see*
Fig. 8).

(c) Making sequences.
Sequences can be made by using entirely *over edge* links.
When these are placed in the body, as spatial progressions,
the corners may be rounded to made curved patterns. Curved
shapes, e.g. HRF-HRB-HLB-HLF, HRF-DRF-DLF-HLF, or

twisted shapes, e.g. HRF-HRB-HLB-DLB and DLF-HLF-HLB-HRB.

The performance of such shapes gives an extremely good body training, particularly for the spine, as the twisting, arching and bending movement required to reach the diagonals is complementary to the more upright way with which much dance training is begun. The actions of opening, closing, rising, falling, advancing and retreating will appear in various orders in over edge transitions, not centrally situated, as in the dimensional cross, but peripherally situated at the edge of the kinesphere.

Sequences can be made using *over plane* links only, when the resultant shapes will be zigzags, e.g. *(a)* HLF-DRF-HRB-DLB, or triangles, *(b)* HLF-DRF-HRB-HLF or *(c)* DRB-HLB-DLF-DRB. In these "over plane" links two spatial properties are involved simultaneoulsy, which in example *(a)* are righting while falling, rising while retreating, falling while lefting, in example *(b)* righting-falling, rising-retreating, advancing-lefting, and in example *(c)* rising-lefting, advancing-falling, retreating-righting. The teacher should encourage the student to translate these lines into their body's spatial progressions, spatial tensions and spatial mass embodiments. They must become dance actions. "Righting" must be resolved into opening or closing or tilting, as must "lefting". Turns, falls, gestures, jumps all contribute to sequences of spatially defined dance.

Sequences on central transitions only involve angular or curved patterns. The following example C-HRF-DLB-C-HLF-C-DRF can be performed either in an angular way or a curved way, the latter being done by rounding the movement as it passes through the centre.

Sequences can be made using over plane, over edge and central links, and these will be found to be more interesting to perform because of the varied use of the body which is required. Example *(a)* HLF-DRF-HRF-DLB gives sharp angles and a different distance to each of the three parts of the whole movement. The last part may feel the most important with the second part like a rebound from the first if performed as whole body actions. Example *(b)* HLF-DRF-HRF-DLB-HLB-HLF would give a contrasting curved return to the starting situation. A sequence using the opposite directions to those in *(b)* would make a good balance as follows: DRB-HLB-DLB-HRF-DRF-DRB.

All these sequences can be performed in reverse and with varying degrees of importance laid on each movement through size and intensity. Students can create their own sequences or master one chosen by the teacher.

(d) Seeing sequences.
Dancing of all kinds uses diagonal and cube orientated actions. They are less obvious to see and perhaps less frequently used than octahedral and dimensional directions, but they are there. It is interesting, and a way of building up a concept of the spatial construction of dance, to search for diagonal embodiments. Dances, sequences and moves made for quite other purposes serve best, so that no preconceived notions of the movements' spatial content are there before the searching. Here is the beginnings of spatial analysis, done by recognising movements which refer to, or are parallel to, the diagonal cross and the cube.

(e) Diagonals of the general space.
The diagonals in the kinesphere are turned with the dancer, and travel through the general space. The diagonals of the general space do not turn. They belong to the room.

Imagine the diagonal cross of reference in the middle of the room. Imagine the diagonals extending to pierce the corners of the room. Less easy to visualise are lines parallel to these, traversing the room from HRF to DLB, or DLF to HRB.

Imagine the cube extended to fill the room. Imagine cubes for each dancer, cubes which are parallel to the one large room-cube. Wherever the dancers face, HRF of the room-cube is constant, HLB is constant. These lines take on new significance when dancing for an audience, for the audience is constant too. Play can be had with using these room or stage diagonals (parallels) and altering the dancer's front. Try dancing from LB to RF, using dimensional orientation of the individual kinespheres, dancing forward and to the right, backward and to the left. Try also dancing with diagonal orientation, DLB to HRF and HLB to DRF. New kinespheric directions will appear with individual bodies.

Notice how dances are made using these ideas. Look at entrances and exits in pieces, or in T.V. dance routines. Notice whether the dances include:

(a) dimensional personal kinesphere orientation;

(b) dimensional general space orientation;

(c) diagonal personal kinesphere orientation;

(d) diagonal general space orientation.

(f) Regular forms.

The cube provides regular forms, not many, but ones which are an essential part of the whole hierarchy. Further information is given in Appendix II.

3. ESTABLISHING THE THREE PLANES

There are twenty-seven basic directions in all, which include six dimensional, eight diagonal, twelve diametral directions and centre. The diametrals are linked by the three planes, the *saggital,* the *frontal* and the *horizontal,* which are also referred to as the *wheel plane,* the *door plane* and the *table plane (see* Fig. 9).

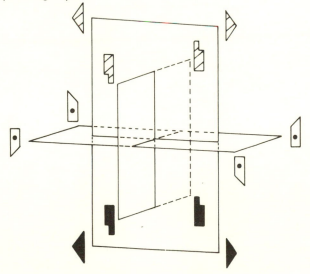

Fig. 9. *The three planes.*

The planes are related to the dimensional cross, in that each one-dimensional line becomes a two-dimensional plane. The planes are not square shaped, but have one dimension longer than the second. The main dimension is dominant, the second one is subsidiary. Logically, the up/down main dimension can combine with either right/left or forward/back as subsidiary. However, the planes are a referential cross for the body in dance. It is evident that one is congruent with human build and the other is not.

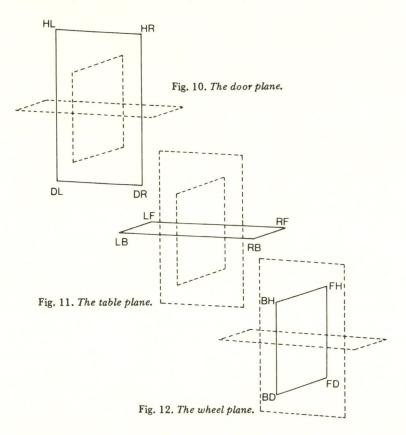

Fig. 10. *The door plane.*

Fig. 11. *The table plane.*

Fig. 12. *The wheel plane.*

Hence:

(i) the door plane develops out of the up/down dimension because of the symmetric build of the body and the ability of the spine to bend laterally;

(ii) the table plane develops out of the right/left dimension through opening and closing properties and the ability of the spine to twist.

(iii) the wheel plane develops out of the forward/backward dimension because the body has upper and lower limbs and the spine can arch and round;

(a) Orientation in the planes.
Each plane, being two-dimensional like a piece of paper, has four corners. These corners are places which are noticeable. Movements in the planes pass through the corners or arrest at the corners, or reach out to them.

Hence:

(i) in the door plane:
high-right, deep-right, deep-left, high-left *(see* Fig. 10);

(ii) in the table plane:
left and right-forward, left and right-backward *(see* Fig. 11).

(iii) in the wheel plane:
forward-high and deep, backward-high and deep *(see* Fig. 12);

The direction ♭ is called high-right and not right-high because it is mostly high and a little to the right. Similarly ♮ is called forward-high because it is mostly forward and a little high, and ♮ is called left-forward and not forward-left for a similar reason.

When *(i) (ii)* and *(iii)* are performed as progression from the centre with the right side of the body leading, the following actions are found:

(i) in the door plane, lifting (opening), lowering (opening), lowering (closing) and lifting (closing), the bracket implying less importance;

(ii) in the wheel plane, advancing (lifting), advancing (opening), lowering (closing) and lifting (closing), the bracket implying less importance;

(iii) in the table plane, closing (advancing), opening (advancing), closing (retreating) and opening (retreating).

The movements may also be performed with the action of the spine particularly in mind, in which case the following appear: bending to the right and left slightly or intensely in the door plane, rounding and arching slightly or intensely in the wheel plane, twisting slightly or intensely in the table plane. Practice should be given in experiencing these movements from all the preceding points of view so that the action and the sensation are both trained.

The planes are linked with the action of travelling, turning and jumping in that movements in the door plane are primarily rising and falling, which leads into elevation, in the wheel plane are advancing and retreating, which leads into travelling, and in the table plane are opening and closing, which leads into turning. Experience should be given of moving in these planes, stressing the dimensional origin and the link with travelling, turning and jumping by giving sequences based on this and by encouraging experimentation, and by looking at dance movements where the planes and the corners are used.

(b) Embodiment of the planes.
The same methods of embodiment pertain here as they do for the dimensional cross and the diagonal cross. The principles are:
    (i) progression along an imagined line;
    (ii) spatial tension between the ends of an imagined line;
    (iii) spatial mass embodiment, the body (parts) becomes the line.

(i), *(ii)* and *(iii)* occur independently or together, concurrently or consecutively.

Hence, for example: the line BH - FD through the wheel plane may occur as:

    (a) A starting position crouched down, rounded in a ball; a step back, lifting, both hands leading extending arms which pass the face, the trunk incurling and leaning back, extending, until a line is made between hands in BH and extended foot FD. In this sequence we have a pole stated, a progression begun by the hands, a body mass statement of the

line emerges, which has tension between the first pole (by a foot) and the second pole (the hands).

(b) A tango rhythm; play between R/L and BH/FD in the arms. Arms out to the sides on beat one with an open step to the right; three steps on the spot, behind, in front, behind as the left arm sweeps up to BH, back of the hand leading, as the right sweeps to FD, also back of the hand leading. Shoulders swing round with arms; hips stay firmly orientated to the front. Repeat, with the same footwork, and alternate arm movements.

This is spatial progression from the dimension to the plane, arrested to create a spatial tension in the plane.

(c) Three dancers, two facing each other holding each other's lower arms, firmly; the third leaps onto their arms, supporting on her tummy. They tip her so that she embodies in her mass the line FD/BH.

Further principles are:
(iv) the directions may be embodied as a whole unit;
(v) or by parts of the body only;
(vi) by gestures of the arm:
  (a) with trunk accompanying;
  (b) with trunk remaining aloof;
  (c) with counter pull in the trunk;
  (d) with the trunk pulling out into the space;
  (e) with the trunk curving into the direction;
  (f) with (a) to (c) in (vii);
(vii) by gestures of the leg:
  (a) extended or contracted;
  (b) across the body or open;
  (c) inturned, outwards, or parallel;
  (d) in jumps or supported;
  (e) with (a) to (c) in (vi);
(viii) by the trunk alone:
  (a) from standing, sitting, kneeling, lying;
  (b) extended, contracted;
  (c) tilting into the direction;
  (d) facing the direction, with twists;

(ix) by isolated small parts:
    (a) hands, head, feet;
    (b) tilting or facing;
 (x) during actions of the whole body:
    (a) turning, including spinning, rolling;
    (b) locomotion, in the direction or counter-direction, or supplementary direction;
    (c) jumping, as take-off, flight gestures, or landing;
    (d) inverting;
    (e) falling;
 (xi) as steps, or support changes:
    (a) with plié (knee bends);
    (b) with relevé (on the toes);
    (c) with kneeling;
    (d) with lying down;
    (e) with sitting;
    (f) with any support combination;
 (xii) with parallel arm and leg use;
(xiii) relating to the direction:
    (a) by penetrating it;
    (b) by surrounding it;
    (c) by going away from it;
    (d) by facing it;
(xiv) the lines may be reversed and transposed.
etc.

A teacher might wish to extend this list with further principles discovered in practical work. However, hopefully, this provides a framework for:

(a) practising and improving and achieving spatial orientation and precision;

(b) problem solving and making with spatial ideas;

(c) searching for and increasing the skill of recognising spatial facts in dance.

(c) The icosahedron.

When all the corners of the planes are joined peripherally a regular body is formed, the *icosahedron* (*see* Fig. 13). The icosahedron is a body with twenty triangular facets joined by twelve corners or apices. It is more spherical than the octahedron and cube, and more nearly akin to the natural

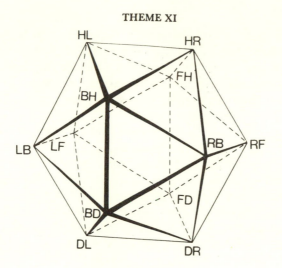

Fig. 13. *The icosahedron.*

shape of the kinesphere. Movements performed with this orientation are therefore sometimes called icosahedral movements or directions. Peripheral lines are made by joining two nearby corners directly. For example:

HR is joined to RF, RB, BH, HL, FH.

This makes five spoke-like lines (Fig. 14). Each apex will be found to have five peripheral lines starting from it, two going towards one plane, two towards the second, and one to another apex on the original plane. All manner of curves, zigzags, twists and circles can be made by linking the corners of the planes peripherally and in order to master these and

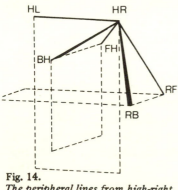

Fig. 14.
The peripheral lines from high-right.

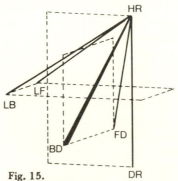

Fig. 15.
The transversal lines from high-right.

make them part of the dancer's vocabulary it is best to proceed in two ways; firstly, to improvise shapes around the body freely and then recognise the corners through which they have passed; and secondly, to consciously join the corners and then recognise the shapes which have been created.

Sequences involving both central and peripheral lines are more satisfying to perform than those with only one type of line, as was mentioned in connection with dimensional and diagonal orientation. The student can create his own sequences and can also master those of the teacher or of another pupil. Work in pairs in the way of matching and mirroring is satisfying and helps to make each person really clear in his orientation. Refer back to the principles for embodiment given in section 2(b) of this chapter.

(d) Transversals.

Transversal links are only found in icosahedral orientation. They are lines which traverse the kinesphere, passing between the centre and the periphery, for example: high-right to backward-deep; forward-high to right-backward. When these planal corners are joined by the shortest distance, a movement of progression passes near the body but does not go through it. The action of the arm when performing this is complex as it will start extended and will partially contract while moving towards the second point and finally extend again. The movement of the trunk is also complex if it follows that of the arm. Central and peripheral links are simple to perform but the transversal ones are more satisfying to the mature person because of their subtlety.

Each corner has five transveral lines starting from it, for example:

HR is joined to DR, BD, LB, LF, FD,

which again makes five spoke-like lines (Fig. 15). Students can find these lines for themselves and there are five from every corner in the icosahedron. It will be found that there are thirty transversal, thirty peripheral, and six central lines.

(e) One-, Two-, and Three-dimensional lines in the icosahedron.

Each plane has two one-dimensional transversals and two one-dimensional peripherals. These are the basic central dimensions of the dimensional cross placed elsewhere in the kinesphere.

H/D is transversally beside the centre, in the door plane.
H/D is peripherally in front and behind, in the wheel plane.
R/L is transversally in front and behind, in the table plane.
R/L is peripherally above and below, in the door plane.
F/B is transversally above and below the centre, in the wheel plane.
F/B is peripherally beside the centre, in the table plane.

Movements orientated to these dimensions are stable and parallel to the architecture surrounding the dancer. They provide a stability necessary to arrest the mobility of much of dancing.

Two-dimensional lines appear in the icosahedron only as diametrals across each plane. The dimensions are unequally loaded. There are no peripheral or transversal two-dimensional lines here as there are in both the octahedron and the cube.

Three-dimensional, or diagonal, lines only exist in the icosahedron as lines which penetrate the eight corner triangular facets. That is, three-dimensional, equally loaded, diagonals, i.e. equally high, right, and forward, etc. However, unequal loading abounds, and these lines are called inclinations (*see* Laban, R. 1966).

(f) Flat, steep and flowing inclinations.
Transversal lines between different planes are called *inclinations* and their character is a combination of dimensional and diagonal flow. Each one is inclined towards a diagonal but does not run parallel to it because one dimension of the diagonal is more stressed than the other two. For example:

⌐⌐ is inclined towards ⌐ but ▷ is more stressed than ⌐ or ⌐
⌐◀ is inclined towards ▮ but ◁ is more stressed than ▮ or ⌐

When the side-side dimension is stressed the line is called *Flat*. There are eight flat inclinations and all go between the door and the table planes and are placed behind or in front of the centre (Fig. 16). They are:

🬀 𝅘, 🬀 𝅗, 🬀 𝅘, 🬀 𝅗   LB-HR, LB-DR, RB-HL, RB-DL.
🬀 𝅘, 🬀 𝅗, 🬀 𝅘, 🬀 𝅗   LF-HR, LF-DR, RF-HL, RF-DL.

Transversal lines which pass between the door and wheel planes have the up-down dimension dominant. For example:

▷ ▮ is inclined towards ▮ but ▮ is more stressed than 🬀 or ◁.

When the up-down dimension is stressed the line is called *Steep*. There are eight steep inclinations and they are placed on either side of the centre (*see* Fig. 17). They are:

▷▮, ▷▮, ▶🬀, ▶🬀   HR-FD, HR-BD, DR-FH, DR-BH.
◁▮, ◁▮, ◀🬀, ◀🬀   HL-FD, HL-BD, DL-FH, DL-BH.

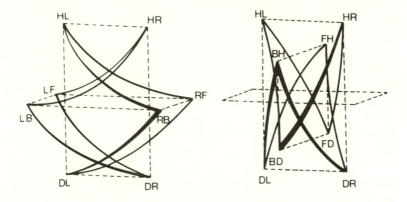

Fig. 16. *Flat inclinations.*   Fig. 17. *Steep inclinations.*

Transversal movements which pass between the table and the wheel planes have the forward-backward dimension stressed. These are called *flowing* inclinations and are placed above or below the body (Fig. 18). They are:

▮🬀, ▮🬀, 🬀🬀, 🬀🬀   FD-LB, FD-RB, FH-LB, FH-RB.
▮🬀, ▮🬀, 🬀🬀, 🬀🬀   BD-LF, BD-RF, BH-LF, BH-RF.

(g) Flat, steep, and flowing embodiment
Flat, steep, and flowing lines are logical forms requiring embodiment in dance movements. Or dance movements may be seen to be the embodiment of flat, steep, and flowing logical forms. The link must be made. Section *(b)*, embodiment of the planes, gives the guidelines (*see* page 126).

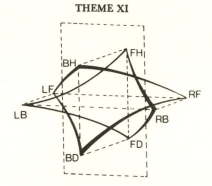

Fig. 18. *Flowing inclinations.*

Progression along the transversal is one way in which these logical forms materialise. It is the most obvious way when starting from the form and developing the move. Progression is usually one body part dominated, performing or following one line in space, of whatever shape. While this can and does happen in dancing, dancing can and does do many other things. It especially produces spatial tensions between the extremities of two limbs, a foot and hand, two arms, or tripartite tensions between two hands and a foot, or two feet and a hand, and even four-part tensions.

These spatial tensions have flat, steep, and flowing properties. Here are examples of positions arrived at which contain spatial tensions:

    (i) Flat: as the landing from a turning jump to the right.

left hand LF	kneeling DR
left knee LF	right hand DR
	trunk leaning DR.

    (ii) Flat: jumped, and immediately mirrored on the other side.

left hand HL	right foot RF
	right arm parallel
	head looking RF.

    (iii) Steep: hopping progression forwards, changing legs.

hands HL, HR	left foot BD
	head dropping to BD.

(iv) Steep:
whole body extended,
left knee and both arms to HR;
left hand holds there.

> right hand pulls to BD to
> support on the floor;
> head BD;
> followed by sustained crumple
> into BD sitting, crunched
> together.

(v) Flowing:
both arms pulling   right foot extended into lunge
LB and RB with   FD.
trunk.

(vi) Flowing: lying, contracting, dissolving into lying again;
lying on the back   head gradually drops BD to
contracting over RF   touch and support on floor
flank to balance on   with arched back.
seat, both legs RF
bent a little; arms
parallel to legs.

Placing flat, steep, and flowing in the body completely as
body mass produces wonderful and very difficult movements
and positions. Many are unstable and need support from a
partner, or appear in flight or as moments which dissolve
into stability. They are sometimes not straight but curved, in
convex or concave shapes. Examples:

(vii) Flowing: performed as an impulsive left turn to
end crouching, bunched together down in DR; right leg BH,
left arm LF, trunk arched, joining BH to LF during the turn.

(viii) Steep: start feet astride upright; right arm H, sharply,
to F and FD on the floor with trunk, back of hand on floor.
Lower head onto hand, left leg bending, left hand placed near
left foot: now, taking weight on hand HL, bend left leg in
completely, gesturing, and extend to make steep line from
head to left foot, inverted.

(ix) Flat: kneeling up, arms lift to cross lower arms in
front of chest, twisting to right so that a line parallel to the
line RB-DL is taken between the two elbows by the lower

arms. The left leg lifts and extends, paralleling the arms; the head focuses near the left foot and turns swiftly to look beyond the right elbow.

All the positions described in this section are taken from dances. They occur as moments in dancing movements. They arrest the eye of the audience and the body of the dancer in memorable spatial tensions and shapes and designs. This is what the teacher is after. The means have been described. The pitfalls lie in being too academic with spatial principles, to the detriment of body placement in dimension and diagonal, or too superficial, to the detriment of the perception system which must have time through repetition to come to know what these things feel like, their syntax, and even their semantic properties.

(h) Rings and regular forms.
Ring is the name given to circuits which return to their starting-point and there are many different ones, but their study is only for the advanced student, for whom this chapter cannot cater. Appendix II outlines the main forms which will be of interest to the advanced student (see p. 201).

CHAPTER 12

Theme XII:
Body, Action, Effort
and Space Affinities

This Theme is concerned with the link between effort and shape in movement and is intended to integrate the work in Themes IX, X and XI. It is the first Theme in which the interrelation in the body of spatial and dynamic aspects of dance are looked at as one. It is the culmination of individual technical ability, prior to learning how to work with a large group, and prior to developing aesthetic and expressive skills and judgement in choreography, which is the work contained in Themes XIV, XV and XVI.

It is presumed that a reasonable mastery of the qualities of movement, as seen in effort and rhythm, has been gained. By this is meant that the dynamic action can be achieved and perceived in either free or metric rhythm, that the dancer can relate effort to sound, or as the interpretation of a suitable idea, and that effort rhythms can be performed in any part of the body or throughout the body, or in any part of a phrase. The task now is to give form to this liveliness.

1. NATURAL AFFINITIES BETWEEN EFFORT, ACTION, AND BODY BEHAVIOUR AND SPATIAL USE

It need hardly be said that a creative dancer may choose to put together any shape with any rhythm, and use any body parts to perform the result. There is freedom to choose.

However, there are certain natural affinities between these factors about which it is helpful to know.

There are two fundamental categories of movement, those which promote flow and those which inhibit flow. The ultimate in flow promotion is continuous outpouring of movement of an expansive emotional type, and the ultimate in flow inhibition is stillness in constrained cool shapes. With every movement made, the way the body is used, the space shaped, the dynamics rhythmicised and the directions orientated fall into one category or the other. Dance composition consists, amongst other things, of clustering movement items from these two categories so that the fascinating marriage between flow promotion and inhibition is presented in a new way.

Concerning the body

Inhibition	Promotion
isolated body parts	body as a whole
symmetry	asymmetry
simultaneous body flow	successive body flow
peripheral guidance	central movements
spatial mass embodiment	trunk involvement
pin body shape	head involvement
wall body shape	
contracted limbs	extended and spread limbs
feet together	feet apart, unevenly supported
fist	

Concerning Actions

Inhibition	Promotion
stillness	travelling
	turning
	jumping
contracting	extending
curling in	spreading out
counter twisting	twisting
supported weight	falling
holding balance	losing balance
gathering	scattering

Concerning Effort and Rhythm

repetitive rhythm	irregular rhythm
duple time	triple time, 5 time
interrupted phrase	continuous phrase
light antigravity force	strong kinetic force
static tension	heavy effort
impact rhythm	impulse rhythm
	swinging
direct effort	flexible effort
wringing	slashing
pressing	flicking
gliding	

Concerning Space

straight lines	curved lines
angular shapes	twisting lines
returning the same way	figure of eight
	continuous line
regular shapes	irregular shapes
backward directions	forward directions
closed directions	open directions
across the body	
small size	large size
focus inward	focus outward
spatial tension	spatial progression
one-dimensional	three-dimensional
peripherals	transversals
	inclinations
inward paths	outward paths
keeping the shape	changing shape

Movement can be said to be actions of the dynamic body related to the environment. In dancing, the environment is not, primarily, filled with objects, but is primarily space. In dancing then, concerns with action, concerns with dynamics, concerns with the body, the concerns with space, cluster. Through the clustering can be seen "schools" of dance, styles of dance, ways of behaving, motifs, choreographer's individuality of mode, each youngster's personal mode.

To promote the flow of movement, or to find examples of flow-promoting movement, one can take one item from the lists under each heading.

Thus:
> actions of isolated body parts, coming to stillness, moving repetitively, and in straight lines, is an example of four-times-over flow inhibiting mode.

also:
> actions of the whole body, travelling, with changing rhythms, over curved pathways, is a four-times-over flow promoting mode.

Again:
> symmetric contracting in duple time making angular shapes inhibits flow.

While:
> asymmetric turning in triple time with twisting shapes promotes flow.

Movements are not entirely promoting or inhibiting. These are poles. Rather, expression comes from movements which contain elements from both sides.

Suppose:
> a wall-like body shape were taken as an inhibiting start; done while holding the position in balance is further inhibiting; but to hold it while overbalancing, tipping, combines promoting (P) with inhibiting (I).

Suppose: the body extends out (P), with inward focus (I);
> or: curved shapes are drawn (P), but small (I);
> or: scattering (P) with static tension (I);
> or: supported on several parts (I) with large (P) trunk movements (P).

2. SPECIFIC EFFORT AFFINITIES

There are links, quite specific ones, between some effort elements and some space patterns, and some body behaviour.

These links or affinities are seen to occur in lyrical dance and in conventional interpersonal behaviour patterns.

(a) *Direct effort* has affinity with straight lines, angularity, peripheral guidance, eye focus, pointed body shapes, the dimensional direction "across", simultaneous body flow, strict adherence to a path, penetrating, monolinear.

(b) *Flexible effort* has affinity with curved and twisted lines, central guidance, successive body flow, twisting actions, wandering focus, rounded body shapes, deviations, dimensional direction "open out", joints evident, surrounding, polylinear.

If all the factors mentioned happen together a very direct expression and a very flexible expression will be seen or felt.

However, interesting and more subtle expressions occur when clusters are made from both. Hence:

(i) a straight line (D) with successive body flow (F);
(ii) a twisted line (F) with strict adherence to the path (D);
(iii) peripheral guidance (D) to a rounded body shape (F);
(iv) joints moving (F) directly across the body (D).

(c) *Strong effort* has affinity with downward directions, palms and fists, contracted, broad stance, bent knees, whole feet on the floor, pelvis involved, large, muscular activity, legs.

(d) *Light effort* has affinity with upward direction, finger tips and wrists, spread body, narrow stance, heels off the floor, chest involvement, small, arms, on the toes.

Here are the two poles. But subtler expressions might be:

(i) heels off (L) with broad stance (S);
(ii) upward direction (L) with fists (S);
(iii) spreading body shape (L) with contracted limbs (S);
(iv) wrists (L) leading downwards (S).

(e) *Sudden effort* has affinity with quick tempo, arriving at a place, spasmic muscular contraction, backward direction, short distance, interrupted shapes, isolated parts, trunk contracting, stepping, jumping.

(f) *Sustained effort* has affinity with slow tempo, going away from a place, forward direction, continuous shapes, long lines, gestural, whole body, trunk arching, breathing.

But look at the expression in:

(i) quick tempo (Sud) and a long line (Sus);
(ii) spasmic muscular tension (Sud) in forward (Sus) trunk (Sus) movement;
(iii) going away from a position (Sus) a short distance (Sud).

(g) *Free flow* has affinity with going on, outwards, whole body, continuous rhythm, large, spread, continuous patterns, turning, travelling, asymmetric, smooth.
(h) *Bound flow* has affinity with stopping, inwards, parts of the body, interrupted rhythm, small, interrupted patterns, balanced, symmetric, jerky.

But:

(i) continuous pattern (F) with interrupted rhythm (B);
(ii) symmetric (B) and outward (F);
(iii) travelling on (F) jerkily (B);
(iv) stopping (B) a turn (F);
(v) spreading (F) but small (B).

In interpersonal behaviour patterns, a use of affinities provides the parties with a feeling of security, of comprehension, normality. When the affinities are partially present or absent, the behaviour can be bewildering or disturbing. An aggressive gesture, fisted, with focus, is clearly thrusting. Everyone knows where they are. An aggressive gesture, with retreating posture followed by a slump, is bewildering. It does not follow the "law" of affinities. It is incomprehensible, worrying. The interaction comes unstuck.

In dance the use of affinities also provides a feeling of security, of normality, of things known. The audience can go to sleep, for the dance is predictably comprehensible. When affinities are partially present or absent, the movement is disturbing. It causes a stir, it is noticeable, it is saying something unusual, it is making links where none were made before in leaps of the creative imagination, it demands response from the audience. It is funny, moving, odd, incomprehensible, bizarre, grotesque, dichotomous.

3. MAKING USE OF AFFINITY KNOWLEDGE

A teacher can make use of affinity knowledge by looking at dances and motifs. A choreographer, in a piece with characters, will probably provide modes for each. Graham's *Appalachian Spring* is a good example. The Preacher, the Four Girls, the Pioneer Woman, the Young Man and the Young Woman all have distinct modes which can be traced as clusters of components. What is also clear in this piece is that when the expression is one of disturbance, the affinities are overridden and abandoned. The Preacher's solo is a clear example. He does expansive movements, with bound flow and interrupted rhythms, with his head involved. He does little steps, many of them, on the knees, very narrow, with wide spread arms and outward focus.

A dance phrase will have several motifs. The motifs will be clusters. They will be flow promoting or flow inhibiting. Looking for these features makes the motif comprehensible, within the grasp of young and aspiring composers. The teacher will help the students to compose, and could use affinity knowledge to aid evaluation.

Motifs that are dull may be found to be over-full of affinities. Motifs that are incoherent may have too few. Knowledge of affinities should help the teacher not only to see and recognise what is happening in terms of analysis, but also to evaluate in terms of clustering of components, in terms of successful making, to communicate through cluster choices.

The teacher will also provide studies for children and students to achieve which contain clusters of affinities and clusters of non-affinities. The materials here for problem-solving tasks, for small invention and exploration tasks are manifold, and obviously so. The teacher needs to do these exercises himself to provide movements, motifs and phrases which embody the modes he has found. These provide the students with valuable examples which they perceive, practise, and technically achieve.

4. TASK SUGGESTIONS

(a) Look at Theme IX — Shapes. Use circles with one arm leading, allowing congruent body behaviour as accompaniment. Identify:

(i) moments of acceleration;

(ii) moments of flexibility;

(iii) successive body flow;

(iv) head involvement;

(v) stronger-lighter rhythm;

(vi) promotion/inhibition of flow:

(b) Look at Theme X. Using jumping, stepping and gesturing:

(i) make the sudden/sustained qualities very evident;

(ii) write the phrase down, using long dashes for sustained and short dashes for sudden, thus:

— — ———— — — ———— — — ———— ————

(iii) thicken the lines where strength is evident;

(iv) identify the shapes used in sustained parts.

(v) identify the directions used in the quicker parts.

(c) Refer to Theme XI. Look at a film of dance, or at another dancer taking part in a class:

(i) identify a horizontal R-L body mass;

(ii) identify its main dynamic;

(iii) identify a wheel plane progression;

(iv) identify the body parts making the progression;

(v) do the movement yourself, and make three variations on it by changing the dynamic rhythm.

(d) Take a theme concerned with the difference between people who get on well together and people who do not. Say, A and B are compatible, but A and C are not. Create two short duos which could communicate the theme. Plan it by processing the character of A in space/dynamic/body/action terms. Plan B to be similar but not the same. Plan C to be different.

CHAPTER 13

Theme XIII:
Elevation

As Laban says, "skips, leaps and jumps are the characteristic actions of dancing". This is so because jumping is one of the first actions of a child when excited, because to overcome gravity is a natural urge, because suspension in the air gives a sensation of freedom, and because the upward direction symbolises human aspirations. Small children jump at first on the spot and on both feet, usually repeating the action several times so that it is like the action of a bouncing ball. The stress of the child's jump is on the enjoyment of the rhythmical repetition of the excited movement. This kind of jump cannot be called elevation but is part of the preparation leading up to it. The content of this Theme is the acquisition of the bodily skill (*see* Cohen S. J. 1974 and Lawson J. 1960 for dance technique; Cratty B. 1973 and Whiting H. T. A. 1975 for skill learning) needed to overcome gravity temporarily, together with the sensation of suspension from the earth-bound quality of everyday movement.

1. GETTING AWAY FROM THE FLOOR

This is the physical aim of elevation. A good exercise to awaken this sensation is to throw the body into the air repeatedly and whenever the feet touch the floor to immediately push off again. The result will be impulsive movements with no shape, and this can be tried first on the spot and then travelling. It is helpful to have phrases that build up to a climax, starting with a small impulse and increasing to a thrust out of the floor, then decreasing, in order to start all over again. This should lessen the strain on the body, as all jumps are energetic and tiring if done with the same intensity over a period. Accompaniment would be no help here as each person's rhythm will vary, having the climaxes when ready.

A common fault in elevation is to strain in an attempt to gain height while in the air. The skill lies in getting the maximum strength at the moment of take-off and retaining only strength that is necessary to achieve the lightness, which gives the body a feeling of freedom.

The actual amount of strength needed is great, not only for the flight, but to hold a shape in the flight, and to control the landing with resilience. Practice is needed to acquire the strength as well as to learn the skilful effort pattern and phrasing.

2. PARTICULAR PARTS OF THE BODY TAKING THE WEIGHT UP INTO THE AIR

It is easy enough to get the feet off the floor but harder to get the weightier parts of the body up. Youngsters who are still growing simply have not got the leg power to lift their increased weight with grace or athleticism. To help in this the focus can be taken away from the legs and other parts made to do some of the work. Leading up with the top of the head has the effect of lifting the head away from resting on the neck, of elongating the neck. It feels as if it were pulling the rest of the body up. Practise this at first with the feet not leaving the floor and then with a jump, repeating the movement several times. One can then try it while travelling, using jumps from one foot to the same and from two feet to one. Still with head leading one can try leaps from one foot to the other with a few steps in between. Practise lifting the chest off the pelvis as well as the head off the shoulders. The lightness achieved helps. A leg swing, or, better, a battement forwards, provides propulsion to lift. Practise lifting up but still retaining a high support, and later swinging the leg to lift into flight.

Parts of the leg can lead, the knees being particularly good for getting height into the jump. Lead with one knee in a hopping action, then in a leaping action, then with both knees together or with one knee after the other in a leap. Lifting the arms over the head increases the difficulty of jumping. It is a superb sight and feeling to leap with wide legs and lifted arms, but it needs enormous strength and skill and joint flexibility. The arms cannot lift or lead the body into elevation, but carrying the arms lightly all helps in general co-ordination. Lifted elbows produce a sharp jump, lifted wrists a soft jump, palms upwards a strong one and finger tips a lighter one. Much practice is needed to co-ordinate the actions of the whole body and the teacher should provide the class with technical training to strengthen the body for elevation, leading to confidence and versatility in jumping.

3. SHAPES AND ELEVATION

Co-ordination of the limbs is aided when the dancer thinks of the shape his body makes while suspended in the air. The body shapes described in Theme IX will be useful. They can be looked for and recognised in jumps and practised. Other more fantastic shapes the individual can invent for himself. Some shapes will be found to help the sensation of elevation and others to hinder. Door plane shapes for better for jumps on the spot, and wheel plane shapes for travelling jumps. While exploring the possibilities of shapes in jumps may be fun and may increase the ideas for dance movements, it will not help in acquiring jumping skill. To that end a selection of elevation phrases using symmetric, asymmetric, on the spot, and travelling jumps should be made and time given to practice. Then the versatility and vocabulary can be made use of in well-performed movements. The shapes made will only be momentary and usually dissolve as soon as the jump is over but some positions can be retained, particularly curled and compact ones. The landing will then be hard but this makes a nice contrast to dissolving the position in a flowing way. The more intricate the movement the less sensation of elevation is the usual pattern of feeling, and it is only with practice that a clearly shaped movement can be unstrained and be really called elevated.

4. EFFORT AND ELEVATION

Sudden effort is needed in elevation, both lightly and strongly sudden. The basic efforts associated are thrusting, slashing, dabbing and flicking. Jumps in each of these qualities can be tried, on the spot, in travelling and turning jumps. Slashing and flicking particularly are felt in turning jumps while thrusting goes together with large jumps and dabbing with smaller ones.

The effort will only appear at the beginning of the flight, during the propulsion in fact. The time dynamic may continue speedy, or it may become sustained as the flight is lengthened in time as much as possible. Floating and gliding can be felt in jumps, producing a quality which is hard to do but most satisfying when achieved. Pressing and wringing are connected with elevation and are a contrast against which the intensity of elevation can be experienced.

Dynamic changes and phrases are inherent in elevation phrases. They can be seen. Basic efforts may appear, but it is likely the flow factor will appear and alter the rhythm and control. Look for time changes, time/weight changes, time/flow changes, time/space changes. Having seen how these look, then start from the quality and work on phrases from that end, finding solutions in the body for dynamic jump ideas.

5. LANDING

Little mention has been made so far of this important part of elevation because, when a whole dance is based on elevation, the landings almost cease to exist, as they become the starting-off point for the next lift. However, it is necessary to practise and experience different ways of coming down. In the main, there are three ways: coming down in order to go up again immediately; coming down and relinquishing all sensation of elevation; coming down and retaining the sensation of elevation.

For the first kind, sensitivity and strength are needed

in the feet, together with a mastery of time changes, that is to say the ability to make sudden impulsive, or rather propulsive, pushes and thrusts with the feet immediately the toes feel contact with the ground.

The second form of landing is the most usual for the beginner. He simply drops into the floor with gravity taking over. It is difficult to jump again after such a landing; it leads naturally into a roll or kneeling or deep support. People who are naturally tense have difficulty with this kind of landing; they come down harshly with tension in the ankles and knees. It is useful to try a roll landing, going straight on down into kneeling and lying and finally into stillness.

The third kind of landing is the hardest and requires both skill and concentration. The transition is between the physical elevation of the jump and the mental elevation of the landing. Every part of the body, especially the trunk, arms, and head, retains the sensation and probably the movement of the lift, except the legs. This gives mastery to the dancer so that the next movement can be of any character he chooses.

6. ELEVATION WITHOUT JUMPING

Elevation defies gravity. Ultimately it leads to flight, but much can be done towards this while still on terra firma. Contrast is a useful method of experiencing any quality and, therefore, to give in to gravity is a good preliminary to fighting against it. There are always two entrees to movement, from sensation to action and from action to sensation. Elevation without jumping is the former. One can try lying on the floor completely relaxed and then lifting one limb from the ground. The tension required to do this, the pulling together of the muscles, is the first feeling of elevation. One can do this with each limb, each part of a limb, the head, the hips, the chest, always giving in to the floor between each lifting action. From sitting and kneeling in a relaxed manner, one can lift the hips up, being aware of the gripping action in the muscles that has to take place; or from standing, one can give in the knees and catch the body before it falls, rising up again. Concentration should be on the difference of effort feeling in the two parts of the action. One can try all the preceding lifting movements with impetus so that the grip required for the elevation of the particular part of the body in question is felt suddenly. The impetus can be gradually increased until flight occurs.

These suggestions may be used by the teacher as a progression of work starting with the mechanics as in (1) and leading up to the sensation in (6), or he may work the other way round.

CHAPTER 14

Theme XIV:
Group feeling and Group
Composition

This Theme is one which will be treated very individually by each teacher. Some teachers, who use their dance work mainly as a means to the personal development of their pupils, may find group feeling an important part of their social development. Other teachers, who stress the art form of dance, with its skill acquisition, and composition making and appreciating components, may find the concept of group awakening almost irrelevant. Some individuals find large group activity repellant, while others enjoy it. Some want to dance in a group for the social experience of it, and others to take part in a group work as performers for others. A skilful teacher may be able to combine the two, which is the ideal compromise, but time-consuming.

1. BEING PART OF A GROUP

Learning the difference beween being a lot of individuals dancing at the same time and being one group is the first hurdle. The teacher should provide the situation. The movements danced should be in unison so that being together, moving as one, is experienced as a timing and vision problem. Peripheral vision is needed to see, out of the corner of the eye, the other dancers. Learning to be really together, to have the same dynamic as everyone, is the key to group unity. Any corps de ballet dancer knows this only too well. Rate of turn is a difficulty, so are jumps, for slight actual differences appear markedly different to an onlooker.

Real unison movement is a unique activity, for even slight differences can spoil the parallel effect. In no other art are people required to conform so rigidly to a common pattern. Even in a choir or an orchestra, moderate individuality, while not encouraged, will not jeopardise the work. Whether youngsters should be subjected to this kind of uniformity is debatable. However it is part of dance art today, and, knowledge of that art as such is part of education. Hence its inclusion under a group feeling Theme.

Group improvisation is the opposite pole on the group behaviour continuum requiring responsive action and reaction, rather than controlling, correction, conformity.

2. LEADING AND ADAPTING IN GROUP IMPROVISATION

Each individual in the group must be a responsible member of it if the group action is to be successful, which means that he must be prepared to lead others through clear movements or to adapt his own movements to the leadership of another person. On every occasion his own movement must be positive. In most beginner groups one finds someone who moves in a negative manner, who simply follows in a passive way, adding nothing to the experience of his colleagues. Each person's group habits (see North M. 1972 and Argyle M. 1967) should be noted by the teacher and situations be given whereby the individual can become aware that he is a constant leader or follower or merely a "passenger" in the group. A simple activity such as travelling towards a series of points of interest as a group will very soon show which roles are naturally taken by the participants.

What also appears is who is a sympathetic leader and who simply pushes himself forward without the necessary consciousness of the effect his action is having on the rest of the group. Some people readily adapt themeselves to the position of leader and they will find that they must be especially positive in their actions, noticing those who do not feel what to do, and giving clear guidance. The following are examples of simple activities which could be used to encourage leader and adapter responsibilities:

(a) A file of people, leader at one end, travelling as a line through the space in the room with changes of direction and level and, later, changes of speed. The leader's role: to make a clear pathway, to stay in each direction sufficiently long for the group to be able to respond to it, to keep a speed which is possible for all with special regard for the last person in the row, to make each level change gradual but definite and to watch his group reactions to his leadership. The follower's role: to watch the leader and respond without delay, to see that his own movements are sufficiently clear so that the one behind him can easily follow. At the first attempt this apparently straightforward activity may well come to grief, with lines clashing and leaders getting lost and the end of the line being rushed off its feet. The teacher could point out bit by bit the necessary roles until a flow develops down the group, rather like a caterpillar. Only then can the group be called a unit and not a line of individuals playing "follow my leader". It may be helpful to start by holding hands and later leave go, but sometimes the tugging that accompanies this makes it more unhelpful.

(b) A loose group, facing different directions, touching lightly hand to hand, or hand to waist or shoulder. Rising and lowering together directly up and down and, later, obliquely up and down. Here no one person is the leader, although the people in the middle of the group are in the most responsible position, but by physical touch a group sensitivity to the timing can be felt. It will be found easiest if the action is very slow to start with until a rhythm is established when the speed can and will automatically increase. In *(a)*, the sensitivity was through the eyes and developed group flow. In *(b)*, the sensitivity is through the touch and develops group rhythm.

(c) A loose group facing the centre, with light touch. The group expands and contracts, losing and regaining touch. Again no one person is the leader but the people in the middle will be the most responsible. Later the same thing could be done while facing different directions and later still, the contraction and expansion could be towards and away from a person on the edge of the group.

(d) *A loose group not touching.* A pulse beat is started and is taken up by the group. The task is to accelerate and decelerate together so that a series of climaxes are brought about. Stamping of the feet will become audible and die down so that the ears, as well as the eyes and general feeling, can aid in the success of this activity.

Having tried these movement exercises out, the teacher will now know who is over-dominant, and who is passive and who is a responsible group member, and he can give individual help. This can be aided by careful selections of the groups for further tasks so that responsible people are well placed in juxtaposition to those less well adapted. The teacher can also join in a weak group, as often the failure is because the degree of sensitivity that can be reached has never been experienced in any form, and he can impart this while moving with the group.

It will be noticed that when children touch or hold hands with one another they tend to lean on their neighbours and clutch them. This is extremely uncomfortable for all concerned and many a good idea has been ruined because too little attention has been paid to this common beginners' fault. Constant reminders that everyone must carry his own weight and not make someone else do it for him are necessary, and movement play ideas can be devised where this really vital mastery is practised. Weightiness or heaviness is a sign of passivity and great steps forward are made when people can dance together holding hands and not be tugging and gripping at their neighbours.

Working with real group feeling is a tiring thing because it demands participation by the entire being; so it is unwise to continue too long on one occasion with this kind of work without giving a chance for freedom of personal idiosyncrasies in between. Without a release of this nature the degree of sensitivity required becomes a bore instead of an exciting experience. A beginner teacher sometimes falls into the trap of expecting a class to regain immediately the group feeling that they had had in a previous lesson. The children might have worked out a phrase together and performed it with real feeling by the end of last lesson, but a great deal will have gone on between the lessons and the phrase repeated after a week's break may well be very ragged; it has been known for a group to be completely involved in their task one week and to find what they had created extremely funny the next. The teacher will have to re-awaken the group feeling several times before the children are impressed by it, and only when the class can be seen to be responding to one another in a more responsible way without reminders can it be said that the group is beginning to develop a social sense. When this degree of group feeling is acquired the act of dancing in unison is "child's play" by comparison.

3. MIMETIC GROUP ACTION

This approach can be used to assist in the development of a feeling for other people and to provide another situation for skilful use of the shared space/time given. What is needed is a scene in which varied activities would take place, an imaginary one for younger people, perhaps "In the Cave of the Magic Fish", or a scene from a musical, or simply a place. The following may serve as an example of a situation in which this kind of work could flourish:

A quay scene. Such actions as hauling, pushing cargo, passing objects from one person to another, chain actions, rolling heavy objects along, gangs for loading and unloading, etc. If the purpose of the activity is to provide a vehicle for group spontaneity, then each small group can be encouraged to evolve its own rhythm and tempo, some travelling and some on the spot. The rhythm could develop metrically, or remain non-metric, by repeating the movements evolved until the character of the rhythm is found. Each group can bring its movement idea out in unison or each member of the group may have an individual movement which fits into the idea. If the purpose is to learn how to perform sensitively and sensibly in a group production, then the moves, or the main themes, should be given by the teacher, the learning being about how to cope with them together. The rhythm can be used so that the main stress is made simultaneously by everyone or so that the various actions have their main stresses on different beats. In the latter, very interesting and intricate group rhythms can be made. Each small group can then try to feel how their action fits into the whole pattern, by such things as "our accent comes just after theirs", or "let's make our downward movement at the same time as their upward one". Finally the whole class will be working as a unit.

4. COMPOSING AND DIRECTING FOR A GROUP

Someone has to watch what is going on and direct events. Possibly this person learns more than anyone else. It is a missed opportunity if this role is always taken by the teacher. Able pupils can learn how to do it.

Begin by placing one youngster "in charge" of each smaller group. He could be responsible for any of the following:

(a) planning the scene with other "directors", explaining the theme, the imposed limitations, the invention required.

(b) space allocation, moments of importance, entrances and exits. If the scene is to be shown, then masking of one group by another must be coped with.

(c) setting the task for his group.

It is a good idea to start with a theme which can be treated rather like a suite. Each smaller group has a brief time as main, even only, dancers, and the second group moves in as they finish, then the third, and so on. Later longer periods of sharing the space can be given.

The "director" is learning to look at what happens, to notice good moments and capture them, to notice poor moments and reject them. He is going to have to learn to put his composition before his dancers, even if some are his friends, and they are going to have to learn that something they have made is a success and another thing is a flop. Something that is good to dance is not always good to look at. Here the teacher will have to decide what his aim is: to develop enjoyment in dancing or develop critical faculties, both within and outside the group, leading to composing (*see* Smith, J. 1976).

5. TIME RELATIONSHIPS

To become really versatile in group adaptation more specific types of contact need to be exercised and experienced. The relationship can be one in which the time factor is all-important, i.e. where the *synchronisation* of similar or contrasted action is brought about. Synchronisation means not only doing things at the same time, at the same rate, but also synchronising different rates and different tempi to make a whole. The following are examples of group situations where the time relationships can be experienced.

(a) A small group, facing inwards. Reach towards the centre and suddenly draw away. The task is to feel together the moment when the sudden action should occur, to synchronise without any outside help. The distance of the dancers from the centre could be varied so that the slow coming together will be at different rates according to the distance from the centre and therefore more difficult to synchronise. The teacher must watch out for over-zealous leaders and others insensitive to the timing of the majority.

(b) The whole class, facing any direction. A common effort rhythm given by the teacher but not a unison movement, e.g. preparation, thrust, slash and recovery. Begin with drum or piano accompaniment to set the tempo and gradually withdraw it so the class continues without an audible aid, i.e. they must continue the synchronisation of their actions by being aware of each other. The same task could be tried with the main efforts of gliding or floating, with a quicker recovery in between. This will be found more difficult as the stress is more subtle.

The following gives an example of a situation in which synchronisation skills can be practised for composition:

(c) The accompaniment is atmospheric and in no way provides a way of keeping together. Visual cues and audible cues must be used, "dancer's counts". These are the way of counting movement time spans which in no way is congruent with the musical count but follows the rhythms and durations of the moves. The basic plan is set up, with floor patterns to be achieved known and the thematic material for the moves known. The questions unanswered are how many, how long for, at what tempo, on what cue? Move it through

with the "director(s)" watching. Moments of synchronised accident will occur, sometimes beautiful. When they do, the "director" must call out. The dancers need to know that they must look around and pick up cues at the sound so that the synchronisation can be found again. After pin-pointing moments which must be synchronised, the quantitative work of counting out or in some other way discerning the duration, number of steps etc. has to be done. More and more synchronised moments will emerge. Many are visually unimportant, but are necessary to achieve the climactic moments. The "director(s)" and the dancers will look for them, count them, cue them and repeat them.

6. SPACE RELATIONSHIPS

When the spatial organisation is the main concern in the group it is the *formations* which are all-important, and as there are so many possibilities a seperate Theme is given to this work (*see* Theme XV).

7. WEIGHT RELATIONSHIPS

The time and space relationships are called synchronisation and formation respectively; the weight relationship is called *consolidation* and can best be experienced through physical touch first. One talks of a "strong bond of friendship" between people and to feel a strong hand-clasp or a firm arm round one's shoulders displays this in a physical way. The relationship is consolidated. When the touch is light it is tentative and in danger of being broken at any time by a slight movement. But to maintain a light contact while moving requires much sensitivity and is therefore more difficult and a progression on firm contact. The following are examples of group situations which use this kind of contact.

(*a*) *A circle*, with arms at shoulder height, slightly bent, linked by the wrist to neighbours on both sides, with some pressure so that a sensation of slightly pulling them towards you is felt. With this pressure, change the grouping by moving towards one another, pulling away from one another, turning the group inside out by passing one after the other through a gap between two people, moving as a unit to another spot in the room. Try the same movement sequence but with little fingers linked only. This will be found to be more difficult and the danger of losing contact increased.

(b) The theme is building a "structure" which emerges on the right of the space (stage) and grows across to disappear on the left. The bits of structure are dancers joined together. Touch, partial support, total support are used. The synchronisation is one move at a time, one change. The consolidation task is that each position arrived at, each structuring, must be capable of being held. The dancers are on stage, or in a place, all the time, lying flat on the floor, as far as possible invisible (lighting?). The one at the right begins by moving to take a firm stance, dancer No. 2 emerges to join herself to No. 1; No 3 emerges and supports on 1 and 2, leaning away from, climbing on to, partially supported. And so forth. At No. 6's emergence, No. 1 retreats to the floor and disappears; then No. 2. The actual quality and style of the moves is at the discretion of the "director". She may ask for sharp angular, stilted moves, or a large travelling, agitated, shiver, or what she wills. The skills and interest are in the construction, the consolidation of the relationships, how to support by what on what, how to lift, how to share the weight, how to come down again. Very young bodies cannot do this, and boys are better suited than girls; but girls can achieve it if there are two lifters to one lifted. Careful supervision is needed.

8. FLOW RELATIONSHIPS

Group relationship in which the flow of movement is felt between people is called *communication*. It is through the inward and outward flow of movement that contact is made, and this is felt very clearly when dancing with someone who uses a great deal of bound flow. It is difficult to contact such a person; he expresses symptomatically the desire to lose contact, not to gain it. But people who lack flow in their movement altogether are the most difficult to dance with. They show no desire either to gain or to lose contact in a communicative way of this kind, although they may be happy to synchronise and consolidate and spatially form together. As has been said, flow means the change between going and stopping, between being ready to pour out or withhold movement. This is the very stuff of relationship, and of all the kinds of contact this is the most behavioural, and not necessarily the most useful artistically. The following situations may prove useful for flow recognitions:

(a) *A loose group.* A movement is started by the person at one end and passed through the group, each person picking it up as it reaches them, so that a wave is felt to pass through the group. The last person then returns the movement back through the group to the initiator. Try this first with free flow, entering into the movement with the whole body and then with bound flow, withholding the centre of the body. The expressions "I wish to communicate" and "I am reluctant to communicate" will be experienced immediately.

(b) *Two groups at opposite ends of the room.* Using a simple to and fro movement get a group flow going and increase the flow so that the movement is passed across the length of the room to the other group who are waiting to receive it. This group then take up the rhythm and increase the flow until they are ready to pass it across. Try also interrupting the flow at the last minute and stopping half-way in the action of passing. The other group will be unable to receive the flow and will have difficulty in retaining contact with one another. The communication between the two will cease and so will the communication between the members of each group.

(c) *Dancing individually near other people.* Dance first with the flow contained in your own body and then with the flow passing through the limbs into space. In the first no opportunities for contact will arise, but in the second everyone will find himself meeting other people at every turn. This flow beyond the limits of the body is essential for any kind of relationship and should be present if the work in the preceding Themes has been mastered.

Flow relationships are about feelings of willingness and reluctance to form a bond. There is nothing in this kind of activity which is skilful or unskilful. It is simply not relevant to relationship skills as is synchronisation. There are therefore no activities to suggest to improve or increase the ability to relate through flow. Examples *(a)* to *(c)* are examples of improvising with it and of coming to know what it is, but not designed to improve the ability. However, one of the differences between a dull dancer and an interesting one is that his/her skills are accompanied by the ability to project flow to an audience and to a partner and in a group. The dancer may not be "feeling" anything, but concentrating on what he has to do, when, where and how. But he is able to simulate feeling through flow, and thence to convey flow to other people.

CHAPTER 15

Theme XV:
Group Formations

Groups have form as well as relationships. The purpose of the forms is to embody the relationships so that the intention of the movement is made clear to the movers, and/or the audience. The forms can also become the intention by being meaningful in themselves to the performers and/or the audience. It is important that the formations are not merely put in for visual satisfaction. They must relate to the content as a whole.

This Theme, like the previous one, will be treated individually by each teacher. Basically their work will be used:

(a) to comprehend the content of forms and/or

(b) to increase the skill of the dancers in performing forms, and improvising forms and/or

(c) to increase youngsters' ability to give form to group compositions and/or

(d) to better appreciate the group forms of compositions seen.

1. THE GROUP ACTING AS A UNIT

It is essential for the group to act as a unit for successful formation play. This may best be felt by translating the movement of one person into a group movement, looking particularly at the shape that the individual body makes. The individual movement should be performed by the teacher and as soon as the method is understood, by a member of each group.

Example one

(a) Individual movement: a curled up position near the
floor, opening out to reach into the direction right-high, with
the right arm leading the left still pointing to the original
spot.

(b) Group movement: all members clustered together
to make the curled up shape, one person leading out followed
by the others gradually rising towards right-high. Only the
leader will end in the high level, the last member being still
low down and the centre person being on medium level,
everyone focused towards the right-high direction.

Example two

(a) Individual movement: curled position on medium
level, both arms leading out simultaneously, one to the right-
high and the other left-deep, pulling away from each other.

(b) Group movement: clustered together on medium level,
two leaders, one moving out to the right-high, the other to
the left-deep, both limbs of the group pulling away from the
centre person who stays on the spot.

Example three

(a) Individual movement, of the hand only: a fist, all
fingers shoot out and gradually close to re-form the fist,
rotate the fist half-turn and shoot the fingers out again,
close slowly and gradually uncurl each finger in turn until
all are pointing upwards together.

(b) Group movement: clustered, shoot out into the fan-
like shape of the fingers, slowly cluster again, rotate the
whole group (not each member separately), shoot out again,
recluster; one after another each member reaches up until all
are lifted in a steeple-like shape.

2. LINEAR GROUP FORMATIONS

(a) Lines. When the leader is at one end of the line and all
follow him, the group action will be linear; travelling in
straight lines and curved pathways will occur. When the
leader is in the middle of the line two wings are formed

which can fold and unfold, in front and behind. If the leader moves forward a V-shaped group will result. When the members of the line are side by side and all move forwards or backwards, there will be no one leader; the formation will have a wall-like expression. It is advisable to link hands when first practising these group movements and to try to keep together without the aid of touch later.

(b) Circles without a leader. A line forms a circle by the member at the end of the line leading in a circular pathway and joining up with the last member. Groups in a circular formation have no one leader but have instead a common focus which is the centre of the circle. The circle can grow and shrink by being drawn towards or away from the centre. The hands and arms of the dancers need to be on the same level in order to create a satisfactory shape and all move really simultaneously. The group can move around the edge of the circle while its size grows and shrinks. Two concentric circles can move in and out of each other, one travelling clockwise and the other anti-clockwise, so that a star-like motion is made. Changes of level will enhance the group shape so that the circle can rise and fall while it travels round or converges on the centre. Concentric circles can have varied levels forming a cone-like shape which could be inverted for variation.

Valuable practice in composition can be had by creating a whole dance built up from changing linear groupings. Different people will have to take the lead according to their position in the group. Draw it on paper first so that each dancer knows where to go. Make it so that the patterns in *(a)* and *(b)* appear. Put it in the framework of an imagined stage or arena. Having got the pattern, decide on the movements, and on the directions the dancers will face. This is the test. The choice of movement must be geared to embodying content, content which is hinted at by the formations themselves. For example, a flat line advancing forwards is the form, the movement danced is skipping — evaluated as an extremely poor choice. What link is there between the formation's content and light little travelling skips, except possibly banality or incongruity? The choice finalises with large, angular, forceful, noisy lunges with arms held on the neighbour's shoulders, boys dancing. The line is made ragged by the boys lunging one after the other, not with flow down the line, but with interrupted rhythm, a difficult task in synchrony. The impression is one of an assault, of a pugnacious kind. The wall-like advancing of the line drawn on the paper is now actual in bodies advancing as a wall.

It is easy to fall into decorative treatment of formation. A circle, into a line, is made pretty by gathering and scattering movements. There is nothing wrong in this as a recreational activity, but it bears little relationship to art.

A group of five is a good number for beginners and the sizes should gradually be increased until the whole class can work as one unit or until a class member is capable of composing for a whole class.

Linear formations of dances seen can be recognised, perhaps drawn. The floor pattern graphs of notation scores of dances can be looked at. All add to the process of coming to know about formations.

3. SOLID GROUP FORMATIONS

Wedge, square, globe, and half-moon shaped groups can be made as well as many others. Each has its own character. The wedge is pointed, has one leader and can split another group. The square is formidable and compact, having a line of leaders, with the possibility of changing the leadership to any of three other lines. The globe has the leader in the centre; it can contact and spread easily, becoming firmer or more vulnerable as it does so. The half-moon is softer; it can encompass another group, can wax and wane and revolve around its own centre. The important point is to make the formation appropriate to the actions or expression and vice versa. This is especially necessary in group dances of a dramatic nature, in that a ritual is connected with circular shapes, attacking with the wedge, defending with the wall, etc. The teacher is advised to bear these things in mind when creating dances for the class and when helping to give form to their improvisations.

4. FRAGMENTED FORMATIONS

Groups can consist of several fragments, indeed they often do. Sixteen dancers become two groups of 3 and two of 5, then one group of 16, two of 8, and four groups of 4. The way in which a group fragments and reforms is part of the composer's skill. Try a unison motif A and a regular blocked formation, dancers equidistant. Stop at an appointed place in motif A, but a group of three who are clustered at one corner perform motif B, merging with the main group again on their last movement. The group continues together, stops, a third group, say a line of 5 diagonally across the main group, make motif C, or B facing in another direction. Merge. The main group continues, stops, a fourth group, this time 2 only, use a rapid travelling motif to shoot in and out, picking up 2 more, and 2 more *en route*. Merge. And so forth. The shapes of the fragments and the movements they are asked to do need to be congruent. The teacher could provide good examples, and one or two youngsters help in the "directing" of the composition.

What is more difficult is fragmentation where all fragments, or at least three, have contrasting motifs simultaneously, especially if they are travelling motifs. But much can be learnt by watching pieces in which this is done. Limón's *Fugue*, composed for Doris Humphrey, is an excellent example on film. Even light-weight dance on T.V. contains some very skilful formation manipulation, easily accessible to youngsters.

Youngsters used to dancing together in small groups can improvise on a fragmentation theme with amazing skill. They are sensitive to each other and know about synchronising, leading, following, imitating. An outside "director", watching what they do can *(a)* learn a lot from them and *(b)* catch beautiful moments, which seem to "say" something, and gradually build up a co-operative piece. Some music of the youngsters' choice is helpful too.

5. IRREGULAR GROUP FORMATIONS

Regular formations are logical. They can be thought out.

Irregular formations arise out of play and improvisation. Start with a focal point. The easiest focus is one member of the group and the best way to learn to build up a group shape is to move one after the other and not simultaneously. For example, one person makes a movement of clear character, rounded and soft, angular and hard, pointed and spiky or broad and steady. One after the other each member attaches himself to the focal figure, keeping in character with him but with personal choice of movements, until a shape is formed. The result may be long and thin, bulbous, compact, with bits jutting out, according to the character of the movement first made. The final formation should be a richer version of the original idea.

The next step is to make the shape simultaneously as a synchronised response to the leader. It will be found that the leader must make a movement of absolute clarity or the group will not know how to respond and the result will be no shape at all but a few bodies in reasonable proximity to one another with no cohesion. It is therefore advisable for the teacher to make the initial movement for the group himself, then help the more spatially gifted student to take over until all the class have grasped what is required of the leader.

Place the focal point outside the group. It will lead to dramatic movement. A point on the floor or in the air or a person outside the group can attract or repel, and this can be used as the starting-off point. The whole group can be attracted towards the focus, using the three levels with differentiations of extension. The reaction can also be mixed, some pulled towards, some away. The patterns formed will be irregular and many exciting and unexpected relationships will occur. The focus can change, can itself move about, or there can be more than one, which will make the formation change constantly. Such exercises are very fruitful in bringing out formations which no one would "think up". A "director" watching can be helpful in forming what is presented in embryo, or messily. Two dancers of different levels fairly near each other can be formed into a unit of two by adjustments, touching, proximity, parallel, unison, etc. Without someone actively forming the responses improvised, the activity remains play. To become a small aesthetic fragment, embodiment in form is essential.

6. VISUAL AIDS FOR FORMATION

The plastic arts give very good examples of formation, particularly modern sculpture where the three-dimensional shapes are helpful. Such sculptors as Moore, Hepworth and Arp give rounded and smooth shapes with concave and convex interest. Boccioni and Larrens give particular twisted and chunky interest. Many linear wire and metal constructions have been made which inspire, as do those made in plastic, perspex and transparent material by Naum Gabo (*see* Giedion-Welcker 1960). Rodin's *Burghers of Calais* give quite another thought, with their realistic expression. The hardness of stone, the plasticity of clay, the smoothness of marble, the jaggedness of metal show dynamics in forms. Many successful dance plays have been inspired by these objects. Forms in nature give good ideas also for irregular and regular formations: landscapes, the sea bed, rock and crystal forms, geological structure, amoeba, the planetary system. There is a wealth of ideas in other subjects on the school curriculum which has not yet been fully explored but would no doubt prove stimulating.

CHAPTER 16

Theme XVI:
Meaning, Expression,
Communication and Embodiment

The aim of the work in this Theme is to integrate and pursue the movement ideas of the preceding Themes and to explore the notion of meaning in human expression.

An audience of some kind is needed to put the powers of expression to the test. Theatre arts are designed for an audience and this includes theatre dance. Painters and sculptors usually have the public in general and posterity as their audience, but in dance in education, an audience of this kind is not always sought because teachers are not always attempting to create works of art. Where there is no audience, the dancer is seeking to be expressive to the other members of the group, to be articulate and to be, himself, the audience of his neighbours' expressiveness. This kind of dance in education is nearer the life than the art situation, for every human being is constantly trying to make himself clear to his neighbours, by words and gestures, which convey his needs, his moods and himself, or to understand someone else.

However, dance in education can well be nearer the art situation than the life situation, if symbol making and communicating is positively sought and taught. The making of dance pieces, the performing of them to an audience and the appreciating of other people's compositions is what it is all about. At this stage, one cannot expect the pieces to be very profound, as an artist becomes an artist by achieving maturity and through lengthy acquaintance with his medium. But the basic skills can be taught, and opportunity be provided for the creative process to begin. The young artist can begin to learn to subject his creations to the laws of his medium and thereby to discipline them through form.

1. MEANING, EXPRESSION AND COMMUNICATION

Meaning, expression and communication are difficult and complex concepts about which much is written worthy of study, but much misunderstood.

For the purposes of dance in education, the essential concept for all to grasp is that meaning, expression and communication through movement in interpersonal interaction is superficially similar but fundamentally different from meaning, expression and communication in the art medium of dance.

Artistic creation and self-expression are not the same. The first is total absorption in the medium, and the second is absorption in self. When it is the self dancing, a confusion can arise. People may feel they are being creative when in fact they are far from making communicable symbols, far from embodying aesthetic experience in form. The word "making" is helpful, much more so than "expressing". That is not to say that self-expressing or improvising with feeling is always valueless and creative embodiment is always valueful. To extremes they could become sentimental indulgence and feelingless form.

The act of communicating is a way of sending messages to each other. The messages have to be coded (*see* Hinde R. A. 1972). They are processed into movements which are the code. The encoder, the person who processes the message, knows the code. The decoder, the person who receives the message, must also know the code. Without this knowledge he is landed with a movement message he cannot re-process, he cannot grasp it or link it with previous experience. It is meaningless.

Code, then, is an important concept, concerning communication of meaning. One's first assumptions are that movement has meaning which the dancer expresses, and this meaning is communicated to the audience. Alternatively, theories of non-representational art suggest that movements have no meaning (*see* Hospers J. 1969 and Osborne H. 1970), and beauty of movement, or joy of moving, is what is communicated.

In interpersonal interaction, the postures and gestures accompanying the words or instead of words have meaning, one assumes, that is expressed by A and communicated by B. But does the movement have meaning? (*see* Birtwhistell R. L. 1970.) Words have meaning. C A T, three letters, is a symbol which refers quite specifically to a domesticated furry animal with four legs, whiskers and a tail, which mews and purrs. C A T is one symbol which refers to one object type. It is called a one-to-one referent. Movements are not one-to-one referential. They are symbols, but not referent symbols (*see* Langer S. K. 1953). An arabesque does not refer to anything specific at all. However, this does not mean that it is meaningless. Dance is called an articulated art form, so is music. Each bit of dance (music) has no meaning, but the context of phrases and structure is built up which is available to perception. A logical structure is perceivable which takes on meaning in that one comprehends its articulation, as one might comprehend the animation of an organic form. If the movements do not hang together, do not form a structure, then they are meaningless. Random movement is such.

Dance, in its art form, communicates then through non-referential symbols, intentionally transmitted, comprehensible in context. Does specific meaning attach to specific behavioural movement? Is there a universal language of movement behaviour, available to everyone, shareable by everyone?

Research leads to the fact that there is not (*see* Birdwhistell R. L. 1970 and Hinde R. A. 1972). All behavioural movement is learnt by the young from their mothers and environment, and young in the Western world learn different movement patterns from young in Asia or the Far East. Hence behavioural movement is a learned code (*see* Bruner J. S. 1973 and Gardner H. 1973).

Therefore in an interplay between A and B, it is now known that they share a code and understand each other's non-verbal cues according to the shared, culturally learned, code. In behaviour the code may be moderately specific. Raised eyebrows indicate interest, a smile indicates a pleasure of some kind, eye aversion indicates a break in contact. Behavioural gestures communicate through culturally learned symbols, intentionally transmitted, but also through symptoms and expressions. Symptoms are unintentional, like spots in measles. We convey symptomatic aggression because we cannot help being aggressive. An expression is something which comes out but is not necessarily in a shared code. It means something to the expressor, but is not necessarily meaningful to anyone else. It is not processed into the shared code of symbols. A is attempting to "say" something, but it is so personal as to be useless as a communication.

The dance teacher has to make up her mind where she stands. Is she going for symbols, or will expression do? Does it matter whether the dance created is communicable, so long as it is meaningful to the creator? Will she take into account the symptomatic movements, try not to see them, or will she train to eradicate them? Will she be concerned for building up structured dances with articulated form, or will she accept expression, as it comes, unformed, uncoded but genuinely given?

The enormous leap that has to be made from behavioural movement to aesthetic dance is a formidable one. There is an uncomfortable middle road where dance is attempted but behaviour allowed, unprocessed, in it. There is another road, where the skills of dance become an end in themselves and the link with behaviour is almost severed and the person within the body is almost hidden. By the sixteenth Theme, the dance teacher's decisions must become evident.

2. CONTENT OF A DANCE COMPOSITION

(*See* Humphrey D. 1959 and Hayes E. R. 1955). In order to be expressive, and to communicate one must have something to express, and herein lies the snag for the unwary dance teacher. The burning question is "what shall I make my dance about?" So often the answer is a story, but there are only a limited number of these which make good jumping-off grounds for dance. Turning to a story is not unnatural; many artists in other fields have gained inspiration from such sources, but by no means all art has a story basis, particularly music and the modern plastic arts. On what then, are these based? On the very material from which the final product will be made; in music on melody, harmony and rhythm; in sculpture on volume and texture of material; in painting on form and colour; in dance on shapes and rhythms. Here we have lyrical dancing, the action and excitement coming from the flow and juxtaposition of varied movement components. At the other extreme is movement which tells a story, which is called mime, and not far removed is dance drama.

In between these poles are shades of treatment just as there are in other arts; Debussy wrote music in which he was inspired by the character of things but was not telling a story in "La Mer" or "Feux d'artifice". His stimuli often had some audible character which gave him the thematic material for his composition and many were moving things. For the dancer the equivalent would be a choreography or dance play inspired by the movement character of some aspect of life. Note that it is not the actual movements but the movement characteristics which will be symbolised.

The key to any form of expression is relationship. It is not one note which makes music, but the relationship of one note to the next, one rhythm to another, one chord to another, one theme to the next. Any story is based on relationships — it is not just Humpty Dumpty, but he and his wall. In Debussy's "La Mer", it is the dialogue of the wind and the sea. A painting is not just light, but light and shade. The relationship is capable of development and the development of the situation provides the structure.

How does relationship apply in dance? The obvious connection is the relationship between two dancers, but that is only one aspect. The relationship of one position to the next, one shape to the next, effort to effort, rhythm to rhythm — these are the starting points for dance. All the material in Themes I—XV is available as thematic material for dance pieces.

3. THE CREATIVE PROCESS

How should the student start? By working it all out on

paper? By improvising? The problem for dances evolving from improvisation and expression is that they are born in feeling. A response to a stimulus, in real feeling, is not necessary before the work can begin. Dances which are made by symbolising are not dependent on feeling at all. They are dependent on total absorption in the medium. There simply must be a movement event, not a hopeful response to a stimulus.

A word on the creative process (*see* Ghiselin B. (ed.) 1952, Koestler A. 1964 and Hudson L. 1966). Firstly, artists work on stored material. They build up gradually and relentlessly fragments of their medium which interest them. These bits inhabit the artist, in what Spender (in Ghiselin B.) calls the "poetic womb". They are waiting, unformed, unlinked. (Herein lies the importance for the young dance composer to immerse himself in movement, to fill his body and eyes with dance, so that meaningful and arresting fragments take root.) Secondly, an opportunity arises, perhaps spontaneously through an idea, but more likely through a request to produce a piece for a specific purpose. (Herein lies the need for the teacher to provide opportunity for specific dance functions, however small.) Thirdly, a state of disquiet commences when the "poetic womb" is fertilised by the idea. A disequilibriating process begins, wherein all the stored bits become available for synthesis, for *creative imagination is the putting together of things hitherto apart.* Fourthly, the speed of this process varies from instantaneous in a genius like Mozart to a lengthy plod in no less a genius like Spender. (Herein lies the need for the teacher to realise that people cannot "create" to order.)

Let us look at an example. Firstly, the stored bits. After much study of several choreographies, the pictures in mind, stored, were an interest in a backcloth of static figures against which moving figures would be seen, an interest in brief spans of dance and stillness, in the activity passing from group to group so that the audience's eye would be led to look from one to the other. Dimensionality against diagonality were absorbing. People influence each other, form bonds and tribes. People change their mode of living through abrasive intercommunication. Secondly, the opportunity: "Five dancers are available for a piece to be put on in four weeks, about ten minutes long." Thirdly, the synthetic process. The disquiet commences and the creative process has begun. What emerged was "Quintet for 4 and 1", containing a synthesis of the floating ideas. No story, no feelings, no response to a stimulus, just a time schedule, and total absorption in the task.

Whether the theme for the dance is about dancing or is about people or nature or a narrative or a mythological story or a nonsense dance, the process of making it is similar:

Stored bits, stirred by an idea into synthesis.

The idea stirs it all, but does not start it all, for a dance is started as soon as movements become experiences and are memorable enough to be stored. They may be movements learnt, movements seen, or made up. These experiences are perceptually received as aesthetic moments. They need not, should not, mean anything, for meaning comes through context and construction. So the same movement may occur in quite different dances, in quite different constructional contexts, and mean something different in each case.

Content, therefore, must have more than one or two strands. It needs several for a stirring and synthesis to take place. It is likely, therefore, that a teacher will work up to "making" over a period of time. He will have several lessons where experiencing through performing, problem-solving, and looking is the goal. Then comes the idea, the spark. Should it be presented as the beginning of the lesson, or at the end of the previous lesson to allow the disquieting stirring to take place alone? If the spark is dependent on atmosphere and feeling being evoked by the teacher, then the beginning of the lesson is the time, preferably a double lesson. If the spark is dependent on setting off two or three children/students only, who will be the choreographers working on their peer dancers, then the end of the lesson is the time, with the teacher available in free time to check progress between the sparking off and the first "making" session (*see* Witkin R. 1974).

4. CHOREOGRAPHIC FORMS

Knowledge of compositional forms helps the dancer to

choreograph his solo or group dances. Below some well-tried forms are described.

(a) The narrative

Here a story unfolds. It should be clearly subdivided into parts: a group start, a solo, a duo, two trios, and a group, for example. The whole merges so that the beginning of each section may not be obvious. The subdivision makes the piece rehearsable. One duo is practised here, a trio there, a solo in the corridor, or after lunch or on the platform. The characters of the narrative will be movement-processed. Let us say "the White King" will have his affinities chosen, and his part worked around those affinities (*see* Theme XII).

(b) The situation

Here the interrelationship of things or people is presented. The story does not develop but facets of it are presented from different points of view. There is no solution. The spatial/dynamic/body/relationship/location/affinities and discords will be sorted out and be shown from the point of view of several different dancers.

(c) Dance by chance

Here, the movement possibilities are set out, the constraints laid down, and the items of chance decided upon. Chance of order according to the toss of a coin before the performance, chance of who is dancing, chance changes occurring during the dancing by cues being given from dancer to dancer, "if I am down then you start sequence 7, if I am jumping, start sequence 2, if I exit you move downstage, but if I move to centre stage, you lie down and stay still, i.e. sequence 3." This is great fun, adding a dimension of insecurity to sequences of movement or instructions which are quite secure. A scheme of this kind of choice/chance making needs to be quite tight. Clarify: location on the stage, whether travelling or not, dominant spatial features such as large or on the floor or 90° body shapes, body part involvement, dynamic range, etc. These cluster into "unit 1", "unit 2", "unit 3", etc., and are allotted to dancers. The method of cueing the change from one unit to another may be wholly decided before the dance begins by the "chance" taking place before commencement. Dice, telephone numbers, clock hands, etc. decide the order of units, duration of units, or retrograde of units. Or the decision may be that Dancer A will cue the duration of unit 1, Dancer B the duration of unit 2, etc., or touching may be decided as a cue to change unit, or lifting, or exiting, for example.

(d) Simple binary form

This is the simplest form possible — it is often referred to as AB form. It consists of a dance with two parts, and very often the second part is developed from some fragment of movement contained in the first. A dance in this form is essentially simple and short as there is insufficient material for long development.

Simple binary form can be used for solo dances or groups. The content may be synthesised from any one or more of the sixteen Themes, and it may have a story.

(e) Ternary form

This is referred to as ABA form. It consists of a dance with two contrasted motifs or subjects, the first being repeated again after the performance of the second. The difference between binary and ternary forms is that the second motif in binary form is usually intimated in the first subject, while in ternary form the second motif is contrasted to the first; changes of mood, effort, tempo, etc., can be made. The relationship of the dancers can alter entirely and then come back to the original. This is a good compositional form for early choreographic efforts, for it works well for solo, duo or small group dances.

(f) Theme and variations

The principle used in this form is that the theme or motif is danced first and then any number of variations made, all of which must retain some aspect of the original. This is an excellent form for the dance as it can be used in both simple or complex ways, according to the ability of the performers and the composer. In music, the usual part of the motif which remains throughout is the melody, the variations being made with tempo, dynamics, use of instruments, metres, moods and keys. In dance this means that the spatial pattern will remain the same with the effort, rhythm, mood, tempo and parts of the body giving variations. In more contemporary musical composition the melody is not always used as the constant factor, but some part of the theme is always retained. This is more helpful in dance, as a constant spatial pattern limits inventiveness. To aid in the making of variations, the following list of possibilities may prove helpful; make the variation by changing the:

active parts of the body, I;
speed, II;
level, III;
size, III;
front, III;
placing of the accent within the phrase, IV;
partner or group formation, V, XV;
partner or group relationship, V, XIV;
body activities, VI;
effort, VII;
shape, IX;
direction, XI;
plane of movement, XI;
number of people dancing, V, XIV, XV.

Change also by symmetric repetition, right/left, forward/ back, up/down repeats, and by retrogradation.

It is not wise to set out to make a theme, out of nothing. This is the road to aridity. Why not take a theme from another dance, one which was inspired and made by a lively synthesis of things stirred? Many a composer has variations on a theme provided by someone else. The theme should be rich, and thinking one out will not do.

Very elementary group patterns can serve as beginning "exercises" in variation making for the young age groups.

The following group patterns as themes have been found useful:

(i) *In threes, one beside the other.* The centre one advances which says, "I go and we part". All turn and travel to the centre which says, "We meet again". All take a few steps backward, "We part". The one who moved first leads a circular path clockwise, the one who was originally on his right following next with the one who was on his left bringing up the rear, which says, "I lead you", "I follow and act as a link between you", and "I follow", until the starting place is gained but in a different order. Repeat. Note that no audience is mentioned and no front stated. The dancing is for each other.

(ii) In threes, one behind the other. All advance. The leader leaps out to the left, then the second one leaps away to the right. The last one travels through the gap made by the other two, who leap in behind him as soon as he has passed. In the new order, all advance. Quite young children can make variations on this theme

These two elementary themes contrast with one, used in fact for a fugue. Here an icosahedric circuit was taken, using spatial mass embodiment and spatial progression and spatial tension, there was a turn, a fall, symmetry and asymmetry, slow tempo and sweeping speedy movements, all controlled in flow. This was rich in thematic material. Progression from elementary variation themes to the complex ones provides ample room for growth and development.

(g) Rondo

The rondo is a development of ternary form. It is referred to as ABACADA form. The principle is that the original motif A is like a chorus with B, C, D being the verses or episodes as they are called. These have quite contrasting characters to each other and to theme A. This can be done in the dance with a whole class theme for A and with individual or small group episodes. This has been used well with percussion instruments, as follows: the theme was accompanied by all the dancers clicking fingers and stamping and clapping. The episodes were each inspired by the sound of a particular percussion instrument and performed by a small group. The clipping, clapping and stamping motif came in between each instrumental episode, so that the problem of picking up and putting down the instruments was overcome.

The motifs B, C, D, etc. may have a chance element, or may be fully choreographed. This form is an excellent way of sharing a piece between different composers, and of giving less gifted composers a little part to make. So also, of course, is "Theme and Variations".

(h) Canon form
This form is more difficult than most. In musical canons one voice or instrument starts a theme, and a second voice joins in during it, and possibly a third as well. The two or three voices are singing different stages of the same melody which go together in a harmonious way. Dance canons have the same constraints. The choice of motif is the difficult part. In dance the points to remember are that the floor patterns of the groups or individuals must not become entangled, and that the parts of the theme must be different in that they show sufficient contrast to be complementary without being so contrasted as to be antipathetical.

It is advisable to deal first with canons for "two voices" which contain a motif with two movement ideas only which are repeatable as in a round. One part is best performed on the spot, and the second with floor pattern so that each participant can easily feel the relationship of the two parts and the audience sees them too. Three- and four-part canons can then be introduced, as trios and quartets, or as three and four groups. A canon which travels through the room is a helpful classroom task, and also advisable to start with so that the problems of floor pattern and number of participants are obviated. Groups of participants can gradually join in from one end of the room. In this way both the experience of performing the canon and the appreciation of it visually are achieved by everyone. The floor patterns can then be made so that the phrase is done continually with groups passing, surrounding and going through one another. The content can again be chosen from any of the sixteen Themes. Note that Theme VIII is useful for a continuous dance on working actions in canon form.

Using the forms
There are other forms, but those described will prove sufficient for most people. Each form can be used on its own; typical examples of each can be made by the class or

experienced by performing one made by the teacher or recognised in pieces provided for appreciation. Two or more forms may be used within one dance. This is usual with *(a)* longer dances which have a narrative character, or *(b)* suites of dances. As an example of *(a)*, part of Milton's *Paradise Lost* was presented as a dance drama. Canon form was used for Satan's army, binary form for the Lake of Fire, rondo form for the building of Satan's palace.

5. CHOREOGRAPHIC DEVICES

(a) Development

In each of the choreographic forms, development is implied. What is it? It is: *(a)* the full expression of something which was formerly only indicated and *(b)*, the arrival of something new as the result of what has occurred.

Organic development takes place when the movement occurrences are allowed to grow in the rhythms of natural phenomena. Waves provide an obvious analogy. The gathering of the body together up and over, wave-like, crashing down, and rushing forwards, drawing backwards, is the wave phrase. Its increase into large stormy waves or its decrease into small wavelets is obvious. Nobody wants to *be* waves. We see a motif which in nature increases in size and ferocity and also decreases in size. Use this development method with a figure 8 swinging movement; it can increase as it repeats, it can decrease as it repeats. Climax and anticlimax will result.

Climaxes produce new dynamics, for growing things increase but do not then reverse the process. They grow into a new state. The bud grows into the flower, which grows into the seedhead and scatters. A movement grows, reaches its climax, perhaps through maximal size or through elevation, and reacts. The maximal size ends in a closed, small position; the elevation ends in a sliding fall. The new emergent movement is the start of the new motif. For example:

(a) A main motif in which vigorous actions were import-

ant, with smooth, slow transitions, could be developed so that the smoothness was enhanced to become a main motif with lively transitions; or, a motif in which a step was present could be developed so that travelling was all-important; or, the gesture of an arm which was an accompaniment to the main motif could be enlarged to form the basis for a second subject.

(b) This happens as the result of some kind of crisis in a phrase. Intense elevation will demand a new theme in which the deep directions are the interest; continuous use of one side of the body will demand balance by use of the other side in another motif; mobility will need stability, sustainment will need suddenness.

This, then, is development according to the natural laws of growing things, natural forces, and action/reaction rhythms. The good thing about it is that the result is felt to be a development. It feels natural. The trouble is that visually it is predictable and hence boring. One might say it has limited artistic value.

(b) Repetition

People like to see movements again. Dancers like to do them again. It is reassuring, it helps the audience to get a grip on the communication code, and it gives structure.

Repetition occurs consecutively and concurrently. If dancer A does the same as dancer B, at the same time, this is regarded as a repetition. It is not a development. The eye of the audience sees the same thing twice. This is reassuring. It shows, through unison, that the choreographer knows what he wants. Seeing it twice makes the choices that went into its structure clearer to all concerned. The same front is necessary, but interest can be had by placing the two dancers close, overlapping, far apart in depth, far in width, on different levels, in the same colour, same but different depth of colour, contrasting colour.

Concurrent repetition, on the other side, makes a symmetric impression. Again look at placing, overlapping, distance, placing on the same spot on the other side of the dance area or stage.

Dancers can face different directions while doing the same thing. Dancing for each other, this works beautifully; dancing for an audience this can prove hazardous. It looks messy, the design is gone.

An audience can tolerate dancers at 90° or 180° to each other, but less than this looks unintentional and indecisive, in the main.

Consecutive repetition by one body can only go on for a short while. The time allowance is as long as it takes for the audience to recognise the sequence and see it through, recognised. Experience tells a composer when that is. Symmetric repetition follows the same rules.

Consecutive repetition by other dancers is always interesting, to a limit. Where they are placed is again vital. Travelling repetitions work well, providing something new with something already seen.

(c) Transposition

Not all movement sequences open themselves to transposing treatment. Those which are spatially based do. High/deep transpositions mean that every spatial curve, line, action upwards is transposed to downwards. FH becomes FD, HR becomes DR, a relevé becomes a plié, arms down become arms up. Right/left transpositions mean that the *pattern* is transposed laterally, but not the body. If it were, it would be a simple symmetric repetition. Instead, HR becomes HL but if HR were open, HL would be closed. Open steps become crossed, croise becomes effacé, open leg gestures cross over. Right/left transposition is not possible for all sequences and patterns, but for many it is. Forward/backward transposition means that FH becomes BH, RF becomes RB, and DLF becomes DLB. Standing in front of a partner, moving in F/B parallel produces this transposition. This choreographic device is more a logical construct than organic growth. An audience may not recognise the dance but will be aware of the similarity of the two sequences, but perhaps not know why.

(d) Reiteration

Once a theme is perceived, repeated and developed, and new material used, it need not be lost. People like to see it again. In a rondo, the theme appears again *in toto*. In reiteration, it appears but not *in toto*, in fragmentation, in a varied but congruent context. Let us take a quartet, with four characters interacting. Near the beginning B has a solo in which she has seven units, performed with no repetitions. Later on she has a second solo. She uses three of the seven units with two other simpler and longer ones and she repeats. She has a duo when none of the seven units are used, but one of the simple long ones is. In her second duo she returns to her seven units, using two that she used in the second solo and one she did not. Her ending position is identical to her start but in a different place in the room.

Reiteration is the reappearance of a motif, unit, movement, pattern, but in a varied context, curtailed or elongated, or the same. It gives much to structure.

6. CHOREOGRAPHY AS A MULTI-MEDIA EVENT

(*see* Ellfeldt L. 1974, Van Praagh P. and Brinson P. 1970 and Cohen S. J. 1974.)

(a) Objects

Dance, on its own, in an empty room, may be thrilling to the movers, but can pall. It is limited in its ability to communicate. Anything which adds spatial height or depth is helpful from time to time. Rostra, wall bars, a hung net, scaffolding, ladders obviously stimulate. Things to disappear behind are good too, a draped chair, a board, a long curtain, a held cloth. Look for the use of these devices in choreographies and try to provide one from time to time for experimentation.

Props, objects can be central to dance. One simple "thing" can be enough to start the stirring of the imagination into new syntheses. Try an umbrella, a Japanese sword, a hat stand, a red disc, a long piece of cloth, a hat, a large piece of black card with a hole in it large enough to get into, a fishing rod.

What do these do to the invention? They should provide a special ingredient so that new syntheses occur. They will provide interest in the audience, initially, but careful handling is needed to avoid banality, especially with hats and umbrellas!

(b) Clothing and costume and lighting
Tights and leotard are basic for girls, with trousers and top for boys who prefer them. A skirt is also useful. Whether dancing for each other or for outsiders, looking good is part of the aesthetic experience. The body is a beautiful object, and, carefully groomed and clothed, it looks better than if it is not. Taking care of the body is a dancer's job, and youngsters should come to know that, whether they wish to take action or not. A balance has to be made, in schools, between taking too much notice of the shapes and proportions of the girls and boys dancing, and not enough. Naturally, if a youngster has obesity problems or has a difficult figure, dwelling on it, exposing the problem in dance will not help him or her. However, ignoring it will not help them either. The dance teacher needs to include the body as part of her teaching brief, just as a string teacher would look after and educate a young violinist in the care of her instrument. Clothing is part of image, and image is part of communication.

Costume is hazardous in dance. Minimal additions are advised, for it is so easy to limit the movement range with a cloak, or long skirt, or drapes, so easy to get caught up. Look at the way in which many dances are simply clothed. Head-dresses tell a lot, so do colours. Single colours make the dancer's body stand out, mottled makes its outline disappear.

Lighting may be unavailable and unnecessary but once in a while a chance to dance with light is stimulating. Shadows appearing, disappearing, shafts, glows, shapes on a back wall, silhouette, can all provide new experiences to store and ideas to begin the stirring of making. Let youngsters see the work of Nikolais. Here is lighting used as more than a choreographic device. His resources will not be available, but it puts their effect into context, it provides a frame of reference.

(c) Dance-drama

The arts favour dramatic themes, representative themes, themes from life, in phases. During any teacher's work span these may be in favour and out of favour. Expressionism favours life themes, constructionism not; so-called "abstract" art forms eschew story themes. But many dances which students will see, do have dramatic or story themes, and many opportunities for dance productions demand them, so whether it is fashionable or not, the teacher should be able to handle them. Boys, especially young boys, love them.

Dance-drama is an excellent medium for work intended to be experienced rather than shown. The real situation, real feelings, can be allowed. The sensate problems, as they are sometimes called (*see* Witkin R. 1974), can give opportunities for youngsters to live through situations which they wish to explore. It may not matter that the role assumed is not communicated. At that time, dance-drama is being used as a vehicle for personal development.

What relationship this has to art is another matter. Dance-dramas for production are full of hazards. The characters must be movement processed; an "action profie" (*see* Rose 1978) of each role needs to be made so that the motion factors, space factors, etc., cluster into characteristics. This demands knowledge and experience, as well as discipline and skill to perform what is decided. There is nearly always a group in a dance drama, a crowd, a cluster, a chorus or such. Their role equally must be processed. The problem of casting will arise. Do you cast according to need or to ability? Do you give all a chance to take the more exciting and exacting roles? Or do you see that the dance-drama has several smaller roles so that each has moments of playing a vital part? But someone has to play the fourth violin; someone has to carry the props off and on. All can help in stage management, in programme printing, in costuming. Provided a place of value is found for all, for which a production gives ample opportunity, the main parts can go to those who will communicate them best, and children comprehend this.

(d) Sound accompaniment

Silence, percussion, words, singing, solo instruments, tape, synthesiser, recorded music, classical, jazz, pop and so on, are all available. Dances which students see will have a large range of sound accompaniment of which they can be made aware. Nothing is precluded and nothing valued as good or bad intrinsically. Context and appropriateness are all. There is no doubt that sound sets the scene; it provides an atmosphere. Classical music tends to give a serious atmosphere, jazz a more relaxed one; singing can take one into a simulated church, watery music into a simulated voyage. Listening to the music which is used on T.V. to set the atmosphere in films will give children an idea of the influence which sound has on an audience. Listen, with eyes shut, and find out how much can be told from the sound accompaniment. Because of this influential power, much care is needed with sound, and much can be learnt by experimenting.

Dances to music, in the Isadora Duncan tradition, are a phase which all dancers have to go through, and, hopefully come out of. The indulgent joy of immersing oneself in the sound and letting the flow of it splurge out in congruent moves is an experience. It is a way of providing bits to store for future use. It is a way of providing oblivion-giving recreation, it has a value in therapy and a value in growing-up. But it is immature dance. It is also unsatisfying, beyond the superficial. Why? Music and dance develop independently. A movement idea stimulated by music will, if it is worth anything, take root and wish to have either organic development or logical structure. Unfortunately the music will have the same need, and so the two media diverge. Rarely, occasionally the two converge.

Again and again, dance fragments from this kind of activity come unstuck. The music is too strong to allow them to develop. Take them, remember them, and allow them to be part of the stirring for quite another dance with quite other music. Do not waste time trying to find a way out of the stickiness.

Most good dance pieces start stirring not from music, but with music as part of the stored material. Youngsters hear music, play it, but do not at that moment dance to it or with it. Later, months or years, as a piece is beginning with themes emerging, the music emerges too. Then the fusion can take place when the movement themes are strongly rooted. The sound can provide durations for happenings already on the way; it can give structure to the shapes and dynamics decided. Remember, the sound accompanies, it is another element. The dance and music need not mirror each other, need not be congruent, some say need not relate at all. However, beginners look for congruity of some kind.

Words are useful for structure. As they need not have pre-arranged durations, they are open to more flexible treatment than music. They can be repeated, be interspersed with silence, with percussion, be sung, be said by a chorus, by individuals, by the dancers. They can set a scene, highlight a climax, be literal, be funny. Sounds that are not words can be used, laughs, grunts, titters, cries, non-vocal sounds, teeth clicks, sighs, all can inspire and accompany.

Dance teachers need to be musically educated. They should be sufficiently literate to be able to follow a score, to read a rhythm, and to recognise a melody. They need to know about time signature, to be able to count music heard, to analyse it into sections, and to recognise repetitions. It is helpful to be able to distinguish instruments, and certainly necessary to be able to provide good sound from several percussion instruments. An ability to sing, moderately, and improvise singing accompaniment is very helpful. Knowledge of style, a basic grip on music history is all helpful. An active interest in listening is rewarding, for accompaniment is a problem, much eased by wide knowledge.

7. FROM EXPRESSION TO EMBODIMENT

Several approaches to the study of expressive movement have been made. These come under the heading of non-verbal communication theories (*see* Hinde R. A. 1972), interpersonal behaviour studies, and social skill acquisition (*see* Argyle M. 1967 and Birdwhistell R. L. 1970). But none are directly related to dance except those stemming from Laban.

Note well, that these studies are of movement not dance, of behaviour patterns not aesthetic embodiment patterns. Is there a difference or is the one simply larger than the other?

The expressionistic school thought the latter was so. They attempted to express ideas, moods, and personalities through enhanced and enlarged behaviour patterns, achieved through feeling the mood of the behaviour and allowing the trained body to dynamically and spatially get the inner feeling out. Choreographies of Laban, Jooss, Wigman, early Humphrey works, early Limón works, to mention a few, are expressionistic. So too are some works from the classical school, which are clearly iconoclastic attempts to enlarge the classical vocabulary. Culberg and Georgi exemplify.

This is expression of feeling, but comprehension of art and art making has progressed a step further through the search for new forms and new modes and new theories. To Langer (*see* Langer S. K. 1953), form is the symbol of feeling, and dance an articulate form of art. She points to symbols, which contain body/dynamic/space syntheses which capture feeling, and through the structure of the dance the symbols take on a life force of their own, are articulate. Reid goes further (*see* Reid L. A. 1969); to him feeling is not symbolised but is processed through the art medium, be it sound, paint, or a dancer's body, into an aesthetic embodiment in the medium, and that embodiment is not an expression of anything at all except itself. It *is*, it *exists*, it is a new *creation*.

This new creation, expressive of itself, is what creative dance is leading up to. Dance in education builds towards this skilful making for those people who are creative, and also provides means of coming to know dance as a performer and through appreciating the aesthetic works and acts of other dancers.

CHAPTER 17

The Relationship between the Sixteen Themes

Each Theme presents material to be learnt, which is discussed in the three areas of performing dance, making dance, and appreciating dance. Most of the sixteen Themes are primarily concerned with one aspect of movement study while others integrate several aspects. They divide into four groups, each containing four Themes, the latter groups being developments of the first and the last Theme in each group stressing integration of some kind.

(a) *Themes primarily concerned with the body:*
There are three such Themes, I and VI, and XIII.
(b) *Themes primarily concerned with dynamics:*
There are three such Themes, II, VII and X.
(c) *Themes primarily concerned with space:*
There are three such Themes, III, IX, XI.
(d) *Themes primarily concerned with social relationships:*
There are three such Themes, V, XIV, XV.
(e) *Integrating Themes:*
Theme IV, combining Themes I-III, while introducing the flow of movement;
Theme VIII, combining Themes V-VII, while introducing working actions;
Theme XII, combining Themes IX-XI;
Theme XVI, combining all the previous Themes.

From the above, the progression of *body* sensitising, body invention, acquisitions of bodily skill can be seen to be: Introduction to the body's range, with kinesthetic sensitising (I). Development of technique in actions (VI). Using the body to mime (VIII). Shape and line in the body (IX). Body behaviour affinities with space and effort and action (XIII). Developing the technique and feeling needed for elevation (XIII). Technique in the service of expression and communication and making (XVI).

The progression of *dynamic* sensitising, dynamic training and invention with dynamics can be seen to be:
Introduction to the weight and time factors of rhythm (II). Weight and time with space and flow in phrases (IX). Basic effort actions as the frame of reference to which dynamic variations refer (VII and VIII). Dynamic rhythms and transitions (X). Effort affinities with body, action, and space (XII). Dynamics in elevation (XIII). Effort and dynamics as an integral part of expression and communication (XVI).

The progression of *spatial* sensitising, training and invention can be seen to be:
Introduction to the kinesphere (III). The space factor exercised in various rhythms through the flow of movement (IV). Shapes and patterns in spatial progression and spatial tension (IX). Directional orientation in the octahedron, cube, and icosahedron (XII). The space factor in elevation (XIII). Shapes and formations of large groups (XV). Space as an integral part of expression and communication (XVI).

The progression of *group* skills and composition can be seen to be:
Adapting to a partner with simple movement (V). Gradual introduction to work in small groups (V Appendix). Learning to be a positive member of, and to direct, a large group (XIV). Studying form in group compositions (XV). The group as an integral part of expression and communication (XVI).

Body, dynamics, space and relationship are gradually studied and trained together. It is impossible to work thoroughly on one aspect irrespective of the other three. The order of the sixteen Themes allows for this, giving a spiral form of development.

The accompanying four diagrams (*see* Figs. 19–22) may help the reader to see this spiral development. In each case the bottom right corner is given to the body stressed Themes (B), the bottom left corner to Themes of relationship to other people (R), the top right corner to dynamics stressed Themes (D) and the top left corner to space stressed Themes (S).

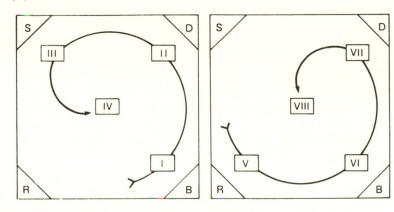

Fig. 19. *Themes I – IV.*   Fig. 20. *Themes V – VIII.*

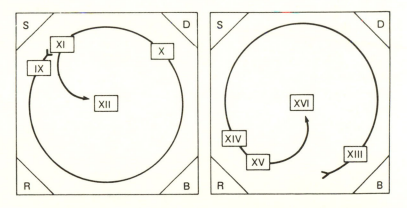

Fig. 21. *Themes IX – XII.*   Fig. 22. *Themes XIII – XVI.*

Reference to Fig. 19 shows that the method of work is: "Build up separate knowledge and skill of body movements, rhythm and spatial movements and then learn to integrate these things through 'flow' ".

From Fig. 20 it will be seen that the method of work here is: "Put into practice what you have already acquired while working with a partner. Increase your bodily skill and your dynamic vocabulary and integrate them in movement based on working actions".

Figure 21 shows the method of work to be: "Concentrate on the form of dancing, using shapes and directions. Increase your mastery of effort and dynamics by learning to make transitions. Integrate these things so that lively movement is given form and formed movement is given life."

Figure 22 states: "Use your movement vocabulary in all forms of elevation. Learn about working together in large groups and use your knowledge of shape to give form to your dance. Integrate all your former work in the art of the Dance".

Figure 23 shows the spiral development when all the Themes are placed in their chronological order.

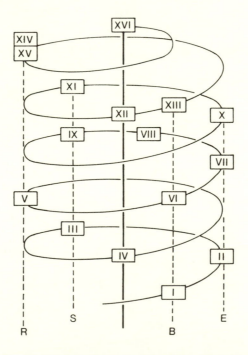

Fig. 23. *Spiral development of the sixteen Themes.*

A Further Statement of
the Theory of Effort

In achieving aesthetic embodiment in art making, the movement bits, ideas, fragments are processed.

They are processed dynamically and spatially. This Appendix shows a dynamic scheme (*see* Laban R. 1960 and North M. 1972) which is a further statement of the theory of effort introduced in Themes II, IV and X.

Effort occurs in phrases. Phrases consist of actions, reactions, preparations, recoveries, repetitions. Each of these may be a one-, two-, three- or four-element combination. The following theory must be read in the light of these facts, so that effort-as-phrasing is pre-supposed throughout.

(i) Two elements
Themes II and IV put forward two-element effort combinations as dynamic modes which could be seen and felt in moments and movements. A relationship exists between these two-motion factors clusters and expression. They have been termed *attitudes,* which may be helpful in behavioural studies and expression studies, and also *incomplete efforts,* which may be helpful in their movement embodiment.

A person who uses the possibilities within the range of weight-flow combinations differs entirely from one who uses the space-time combinations. At one time, or under certain circumstances, a person is more likely to stay within the four possible variants of weight-flow, than he is to switch from weight-flow to space-time. He may have light/strong/heavy variety with flow changes, but does not display clear time changes nor marked spatial polarity. The range of each person is coloured in such a way that it is recognisable as a mode in which variations are made. Words to describe these attitudes are very difficult to find, there being none which are really suitable, but "dream-like" and "awake" were chosen.

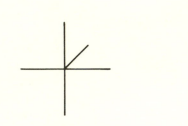

DREAM-LIKE   AWAKE

The "awake" mode consists of clarity in the "here and now", in the space and time, manifest in four variants:

(a) sudden flexible;
(b) sudden direct;
(c) sustained flexible;
(d) sustained direct.

Referring to the affinities in Theme XII, these can be seen to appear in movement in many guises, of which the following are examples:

(a_1) a twisting, quick arrival;
(b_1) a straight, speedy step;
(c_1) continuous surrounding;
(d_1) a legato focused forward gesture.

The "dream like" mode concentrates on the body sensation of strong/light/with occasional heaviness, with the emotionality of flow in the variants:

(a) strong free;
(b) light free;
(c) strong bound;
(d) light bound.

Referring, again, to the affinities in Theme XII, we find the following possibilities:

(a_1) muscular fluidity from limb to limb;
(b_1) rising and turning, on and on;
(c_1) deep held contracted positions;
(d_1) balancing on the toes.

Heavy weight use may occur momentarily too, in swinging and flopping.

The choice of dynamic clusters expresses and communicates a mode of behaviour $(a)-(d)$. The movements which are needed to transform this into an aesthetic symbol of dynamic clusters are dance movements $(a_1)-(d_1)$. They are expressive of themselves in a way that, through construction, repetition, reiteration, etc., becomes meaningful.

MOBILE   STABLE

The "stable" mode concentrates on body sensation (as did "dream-like"), but synthesised with spatial clarity. The epitome of this mode in movements is statue-like shapes, twisted round or angular or straight, dimensional or diagonal, done with delicacy (as in a filigree) or done with solidity (as in stone and concrete).

The "mobile" mode contrasts with stability utterly. Emotional involvement in flow inhibition and abandon appears with sudden bursts or sustainment.

Examples of words which conjure the dynamic sensation and impression serve to exemplify:

(a) sudden free	could be	overflowing excitement;
(b) sudden bound	could be	spasmic rigidity;
(c) sustained free	could be	endless abandon;
(d) sustained bound	could be	long-drawn-out caution.

Changes from within one attitude provide the mode. Visualise the lack of spatial clarity in the mobile mode compared with the stable; consider the dynamic moving variety compared with the relatively stationary stable mode. Consider the muscular unemotional activity of stable and the emotional nervousness of the mobile.

The "near" mode combines bodily sensation with time changes. It appears as rhythmic, percussive, variety of a haptic kind:

(a) light sudden;
(b) strong sudden;
(c) light sustained;
(d) strong sustained.

These could be roughly translated into musical instructions:

(a_1) staccato;
(b_1) marcato;
(c_1) legato;
(d_1) maestoso.

Shape is irrelevant, direction is irrelevant (space), so is fluidity and caution (flow).

But what a contrast there is in the *remote* mode. Here are:

(a) direct free;
(b) flexible free;
(c) direct bound;
(d) flexible bound.

Referring again to the affinities (*see* Theme XII), we find the following examples of movements:

(a_1) monolinear outward gestures;
(b_1) progression along spiralling lines;
(c_1) interruptions in angular shapes;
(d_1) uneven wandering patterns.

Try combining actions (a_1)–(d_1) with the following dynamic feeling-words for the same effort qualities:

(a_2) pouring out towards a goal;

(b₂) with easy carelessness;
(c₂) precisely witheld;
(d₂) in a restricted sphere.

These are actions with dynamic feeling in the remote mode.

(ii) Three elements, known as drives
These are three-motion-factor combinations and there are four kinds: weight-space-time combinations which are called effort actions, which are the basis described earlier, weight-space-flow combinations which are called "passionate" effort, weight-space-flow combinations which are called "spell-like" effort, and space-time-flow combinations which are called "visionary" effort.

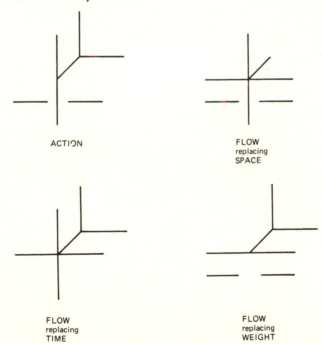

ACTION

FLOW
replacing
SPACE

FLOW
replacing
TIME

FLOW
replacing
WEIGHT

Again, it must be said that these words are only attempts to describe in words states of mind and body which are indescribable in anything but technical language. What these drives show in movement is the replacement of one of the motion factors of the basic effort actions by the flow factor.

Passionate effort is essentially part of dance, but visionary and spell-like are more likely to occur, recognisably, in the behavioural context as they lack rhythmicality which is a usual feature of dance.

Passionate effort was included in Theme X, although not mentioned by name, as basic efforts with spatial clarity replaced by flow quality. It is helpful in the dance context to see passionate effort stemming from the effort attitudes.

When the mobile and the dream-like modes synthesise, passionate effort results. Combining *(a)–(d)* of both, eight variants occur:

(a) strong free sudden;
(b) strong free sustained;
(c) strong bound sudden;
(d) strong bound sustained;
(e) light free sudden;
(f) light free sustained;
(g) light bound sudden;
(h) light bound sustained.

In passionate effort the space element is replaced by either free flow or bound flow, so that a passionate thrust is firm and sudden but the directness is replaced by, say, bound flow. The movement loses its aimed quality and becomes restricted; instead of being positively controlled spatially in pathway and goal, the bound flow inhibits the spatial manifestation so that spasmic bursts result. A passionate floating effort is light sustained and free flow, the flexibility having dissolved into fluidity. The presence of flow in the movement means that one of the elements necessary for efficient action in our mass/space/time environment is lacking, and in this case it is the control of space.

Referring again to the affinities in Theme XII and the examples of mobile and dream-like, we find movement examples such as:

(*a* and *b*) muscular fluidity from limb to limb (strong free) with overflowing excitement (free sudden), or with endless abandon (free sustained);

(*c* and *d*) rising and turning, on and on (light free), also with overflowing excitement, or endless abandon;

(e and f) deep held contracted positions (bound strong), with spasmic rigidity (bound sudden), or moved with long-drawn-out caution (bound sustained);

(g and h) balancing on the toes (bound light), also with spasmic rigidity or with long-drawn-out caution.

Looked at another way, passionate effort appears when the near mode synthesises with flow quality. Refer back; there will be:

(a_2) staccato movements becoming bouncy with free flow;
(b_2) staccato movements becoming jerky with bound flow;
(c_2) marcato movement becoming boisterous with free flow;
(d_2) marcato movement becoming percussive with bound flow;
(e_2) legato movement becoming sentimental with free flow;
(f_2) legato movement becoming constricted with bound flow;
(g_2) maestoso movement becoming appassionato with free flow;
(h_2) maestoso movement becoming grating and growling with bound flow.

A dance, in the passionate style throughout, is a disaster, artistically speaking. It is spatially a non-starter. However, some rites and rituals, much jiving and disco dancing, is exactly this. Form is unimportant; bodily feeling and emotional involvement is all. However, much good dancing which does have some form, includes this effort style. Some folk dance idioms do. Spanish, for example, shows abandon and restraint (flow) with very intricate rhythmic excitement (weight/time). There are patterns too, but also moments and movements where the dynamic content overrides the spatial content, which dissolves into fluidity and interruption.

In spatially structured dances, the coolness of controlled pattern is beautifully countered by passionate effort, which puts the other picture of dance forward. The flow-inhibiting structure and the flow-promoting passionate dynamic synthesise in phrases of enormous interest.

In spell-like effort the time element is replaced by flow, so that a slash in this drive could be shown as a firm-flexible-bound flow movement, the suddenness having dissolved, producing a knotted quality. Spell-like efforts are so called because the lack of time control makes the actions unrhythmic and indecisive. The intuitive powers of the person seem weakened so that normally quick reactions to stimuli do not materialise. In this state, objective action which requires exact timing is not accurate, as the essential awareness of time has been replaced by bound flow which restricts the decisiveness of the movement. A spell-like gliding effort may be shown as light, direct and free flow, the sustainment having disappeared. A person who is showing this lacks a sense of timing, which may mean that he is, at that moment, unable to synchronise his movement with that of another person or object. This drive can be used in dance symbols, but is not often. A timelessness may well be given to one dancer to distinguish him from the rhythmical group.

A visionary effort is one in which the weight factor is replaced by the flow factor, the consciousness of or concern with the body's tension is replaced by flow changes. A pressing effort action in this state may be seen as a direct-sustained-bound flow movement, the firm tension having been replaced by restriction of the flow. A visionary flicking effort could contain flexible-sudden-free flow qualities, the light having been replaced by fluidity. A person in this state is unconcerned for himself and his body, and his movements reflect a lack of tactile control. The rise and fall associated with light/strong movement is lacking in this drive, the moves tending to be more or less horizontal. No touching, changes of support, heaviness, or lifts occur. Remote and awake may synthesise in this drive, or awake and mobile, or mobile and remote. Reference to the affinities in Theme XII will provide possible movement examples.

The content of this Appendix is not easy stuff for students to grasp. But artistic symbol making and symbol recognition and symbol performing are so exciting once the breakthrough is made into processing feeling and expression into movement bits and clusters ready to be synthesised.

A Further Statement of the Theory of Space

In achieving aesthetic embodiment in art making, the movements, bits, ideas, and fragments are processed. They are processed dynamically and spatially. This Appendix outlines a spatial scheme (*see* Laban R. 1966) which is a further statement of the theory of space introduced in Themes III, IX and XI.

The comprehensive study of spatial form in the kinesphere is called *choreutics*. It includes the spatial organisation of the kinesphere and the way in which the logical forms, found in this organisation, materialise in the dancer's body.

Choreutic forms were conceived by Rudolf Laban. They constitute theoretical models from which analysis of the kinesphere can be made. The forms materialise in the body in spatially clear movements and can be seen to occur in choreographic works of a wide variety of style.

This study has been compared analogously to the study of musical harmony. There is a similarity which cannot be ignored for the twelve notes of the octave can compare with the twelve spatial locations of the icosahedron. A congruency exists. Choreutics has been called the study of "Space Harmony". The word "harmony" conjures up thoughts of harmonious movements, and indeed harmonious properties were suggested for choreutic forms by Laban. In this book the term "choreutic" is used and no suggestion of "harmonious" properties is posited. On the contrary the forms are seen in a linguistic framework.

1. LOGICAL FORM AND BODY UTTERANCE

Choreutic forms are spatial structures which have syntactic significance. The syntax of movement, its grammar, is governed by rules which can readily be seen to refer to spatial organisation. This organisation provides "logical forms". This term is used in linguistic study (*see* Lyons J. 1968) to distinguish the utterances of speech from the logical form of what is uttered. Prosodics is the name given to the manner in which the utterance is delivered. One cannot fail to see how the prosodic studies of verbal language are analogous to the effort and dynamic studies of dance, that vocal utterance in speech is to body movements in dance, and that logical form in language is to spatial organisation in dance, all analogous.

Therefore to comprehend choreutics one must see the forms in two distinct guises:

(a) as logical forms, disembodied structural forms related to the three-dimensional regular forms, the octahedron, cube, and icosahedron;

(b) as body utterances, embodied in movements in the kinesphere, referring to the logical forms.

The significance of this distinction is that the movements in which the forms materialise are recognised as having total freedom of expression, subject only to the purpose for which they are made.

The style with which choreutic scales and rings was introduced by Laban, and thence used by his direct students, can be seen in historical context. They have evident stylistic restraints:

(a) they were performed by the whole body as one congruent unit;

(b) the spatial pattern was followed by one limb and the rest of the body organised to enhance the spatial properties of that limb's pattern;

(c) the second body side acted in opposition to the main pattern-following side;

(d) the trunk acted by following the patterns, either moving with or against the leading limb;

(e) steps were congruent with the pattern, again either with or against.

This fluid, simple unity of performance was the dominant style in which the forms were danced, at any rate in studies and class work. Now it can be seen as one of many other possible ways. Pointers to those ways are outlined in Theme XI section 3 *(b)* "Embodiment of the planes", and the creative process of each composer will provide the synthesis.

A completely free choice of body use would produce chaotic novelty. Aesthetic criteria are needed as constraints and incentives, so that notions of articulate structure, unity of form would constrain, and the need to explore affinities would provide incentive. Questions of view point would encourage change of front, for an audience looks from one place, normally. Forward/backward movements, seen head-on, are unimpressive, but looking from the side provides access to their content.

Because of this freedom of body utterance, one is able to look for the logical forms in all dance. Choreographic works of wide stylistic difference undoubtedly include them, in fragmented form, as will be seen later.

2. THE FORMS

There are literally thousands. A sampling is given, which serves to show the organisation, and progression from simple triangular form to interrelated seven-part and twelve-part figures:

1. Octahedral Forms:

      (i) dimensional cross;
      (ii) three-rings;
      (iii) six-rings;
      (iv) twelve-rings.

2. Cubic Forms:

      (i) diagonal cross;
      (ii) three-rings;
      (iii) six-rings;
      (iv) twelve-rings.

3. Icosahedral Forms:

(a) with diagonal axes:

(i) primary scales;
(ii) three-rings, peripheral and transversal;
(iii) four-rings, plane and twisted;
(iv) six-rings, axis and equator scales;
(v) twelve-rings, transversal, "A" and "B" scales;
(vi) seven-rings, mixed transversal and peripheral;

(b) with axes through corners:

(i) five-rings;
(ii) seven-rings, peripheral.

In addition to these, which are forms published by Laban, there are two sets more which complement them, which he either partially ignored or was not aware of:

(c) with diametral axes:

(i) primary scales;
(ii) three-rings, peripheral and transversal;
(iii) four-rings;
(iv) six-rings;
(v) twelve-rings;
(vi) seven-rings, mixed;

(d) with diagonal axes, twisted:

(i) primary scales;
(ii) four-rings;
(iii) twelve-rings.

These last two provide stable one-dimensional forms, which provide a balance to a mobile inclinational forms in 3 (a) and 3 (b).

EXAMPLES:

Example (i) Octahedral Six-rings

(a) Logical form

How many?	4
How subdivided?	1 per diagonal
How many segments?	6
How grouped?	3 + 3
Relation to centre	Peripheral
Quality of segments	Two-dimensional
Axis	One diagonal
Balance	Within itself, 1/2:1/2 complementary
Shape	Zigzag circuit
Situation	Around the centre of the kinesphere.

Example around HLB/DRF (*see* Fig. 24): commencing in this case at R, but any starting point may be taken, the circuit is: R – H – F – L – D – B – R.

Looking at every second situation, two triangles (three-rings) can be seen: R – F – D – R and H – L – B – H. The axis pierces these two triangles, and the six-ring travels between the two triangles.

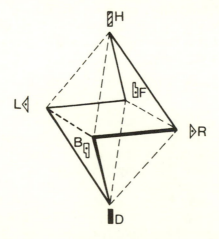

Fig. 24. *A six-ring.*

The second three lines are totally complementary to the first three lines, thus:

$$R - H - R - L$$
$$L - D - B - R$$

There are four six-rings, one around each diagonal axis. They are easily found by transposing. Hence:

(*i*) R—L transposition gives $L - H - F - R - D - B - L$;
(*ii*) H—D transposition gives $R - D - F - L - H - B - R$;
(*iii*) F—B transposition gives $R - H - B - L - D - F - R$.

(b) Body utterance of an octahedral six-ring.

The first question to be answered is, "For whom is the body utterance?" Is it for the enjoyment/aesthetic experience of the dancer, or is it for the enjoyment/aesthetic experience of an onlooker? Whichever answer is affirmative, the utterance must essentially be different and geared to the purpose decided. If for the dancer, and a fairly beginner one at that, then a simple whole body congruity would suffice, using spatial progression along the lines led by the right arm, repeated on the left side. The moves from R to H to F offer no problems. F to L requires crossing over arm gestures and a decision whether to step across with the right foot or open with the left foot. For L to D the support may be in deep plié or in kneeling, on either knee. In D to B the arm either continues across to B, with a sharp twist left of the trunk, or to open B with a twist right. B to R follows from that. A useful support rhythm is:

r foot	both	r foot	l foot	both	l foot	r foot
R	H	F	L	D	B	R

The line from one location to the next may remain peripheral, in which case hand and wrist utterance can be of interest. But the line may be taken as loops passing near the centre of the body, swooping in and out.

Alternating gathering and scattering is pleasant to do, and can be done to make more rounded the peripheral arcs from one situation to another. The gathering palm and the opening back of the hand alternate leadership.

Jumping, travelling forward, and turning left go well, in

that order, starting from R. From L, falling, travelling back-wards, and turning R is the order.

Try dancing it as a counter-tension sequence with a partner.

(i)	R –	H –	F –	L –	D –	B –	R;
counter direction	l	d	b	r	h	f	l;
(ii)	L –	D –	B –	R –	H –	F –	L;
counter direction	r	h	f	l	d	b	r.

If A and B conceive of centre as the spot between them, then they will reach across to meet each other and by half way will have changed places. On H/D they will be *on* the centre, creating a spatial tension between H and D.

If, however, the body utterance is for an audience, then several major steps have to be taken. Examples are:

(i) the six-ring need not be performed *in toto*; fragments may be used instead, and repetition, reiteration and develop-ment may all take place;

(ii) the front for each movement will be organised so that the audience may appreciate its properties;

(iii) the line R–L may run through the shoulder girdle for arm gestures, and through hip girdle for leg gestures, so that parallel arms and legs are seen against an upright trunk;

(iv) spatial mass may be used to make highly visual the dimensional links between locations. The locations could be lost and the lines uttered unlocated. Hence a tilted arabesque HB/DF will communicate H–F, and a horizontal arabesque BL–FR will show the line F–L. Partner support could be used, and a structure of scaffolding has been used on to which dancers climbed; by holding on with different parts of their bodies, these spatial mass tensions are shown most excitingly;

(v) the six-ring has been used as a spatial structure on which to base a fight sequence. The six-ring was seen in the axes of the general space so that F = downstage, R and L = wingwards, etc. It could, of course, be orientated to a stage corner. F could be a downstage corner, etc. The utterance

was full of transitions and had pugnacious dynamics for the spatial structure which provided the syntax;

(vi) part two of the six-ring has provided an entrance motif:

L — D: roll curled in, onto knees (spatial progression);

D — B: lean from knees to head BH, hands by shoulders (spatial mass);

B — R ⎫R step, torso in F, arms R and L, left leg parallel

R — L:⎭to arms (progression into mass);

      repeat.

Example (ii) Transveral three-rings

(a) Logical form

How many?	8
How subdivided?	2 per diagonal
How many segments?	3
How grouped?	Equal
Relation to centre	Transversal
Quality of segments	Diagonal inclinations
Axis	One equal diagonal
Balance	*(a)* within itself as three contrasts
	(b) counterbalanced by its opposite ring
Shape	Triangle
Situation	Around the centre.

The three-rings are:

	or	hr, bd, lf, hr.
	or	dl, fh, rb, dl.
	or	hr, fd, lb, hr.
	or	dl, bh, rf, dl.
	or	hl, bd, rf, hl.
	or	dr, fh, lb, dr.
	or	hl, fd, rb, hl.
	or	dr, bh, lf, dr.

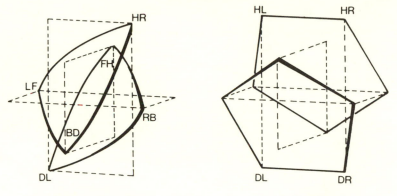

Fig. 25. *Two three-rings.*   Fig. 26. *Two five-rings.*

Each one can be seen as three single units or three double units. The double units are *volutes*, that is two transversals on different diagonals.

(i) HR − BD (steep on diagonal DLB);
(ii) BD − LF (flowing on diagonal HLF);
(iii) LF − HR (flat on diagonal HRB).

The volutes form sweeping curves, starting at one location, passing through the second, and ending at the third. Hence:

(i) HR − (BD) − LF;
(ii) LF − (HR) − BD;
(iii) BD − (LF) − HR.

They can be seen as a *chord*, three spokes coming from a centre simultaneously.

Note that each pair are entirely complementary to each other, and have a common axis through their centres. The two shown in Fig. 25 have DRF and HLB as their axis.

(b) Body utterance of three-rings.
When the performance is for the dancer, then the contrasting whole body actions are meaningful. Taking one of the two rings shown in Fig. 25 and starting in the table plane, the following properties pertain to the locations arrived at and to the inclination between them, first when the right body side leads, and second when the left leads.

LF	to	HR	to	BD	to	LF
closed (forwards)	opening	lifted (open)	lowering	retreated (back)	advancing	closed (forwards)
open (forwards)	closing	lifted (closed)	lowering	retreated (back)	advancing	open (forwards)

These feel most enjoyable, and give a sense of the body in space with dynamic action. They may not look anything, spatially, to an audience, except dynamically fluid.

Maximum congruency is experienced when the legs behave thus:

start	*gesture*	*step*
r steps LF across in front	(l behind and across)	r relevé HR,
	(l backwards bending)	r deep plié BD or kneel deep,
	(l forward and l rising a bit)	r across LF.

The congruency in the trunk is leaning away from the notional centre, which is between the three locations. Hence:

(i) LF is leaning, the chest more or less horizontally LF;

(ii) HR is tilted over, pulling the spine up and opening the chest;

(iii) BD is arching backwards as much as possible, twisting the chest to the right to accommodate the arm BD. To increase the flow, allow the head to follow the line of the spine; to decrease it, hold the head more vertical.

When volutes are wanted then the two lines are joined in one move. It is helpful then to leg gesture into the location passed through, and to step into the location arrived at. Starting from the door plane:

(i) HR is an open arabesque tension between HR and DL;

(ii) (BD): step left plié, right leg bent, gestures to BD and right arm also forming a circular shape momentarily, body arching (twisted) back;

(iii) LF swing through to step right into a crossed arabesque LF–RB;

(iv) (HR): step l, right leg gesturing HR, extended if possible, if not then HR from the knee, as a rond de jambe, right arm sweeping round too;

(v) BD complete rond de jambe to step BD in plié, arm BD;

(vi) (LF): step LF with left foot sweeping right arm and leg through LF to open HR and step HR.

This can be done with one volute at a time, with a transition on the other body side. Or with an extra step at LF to end on the left foot with open left arm, the next volute being done with left side leading, transferring back onto the right for the third volute.

When the utterance is for an audience, then their appreciation is what provides the constraints and incentives to the manner of performance.

(i) The ring can be flattened into a straight line, and used as a locomotor pattern, with one high one deep and one medium level stress, turning so that the direction of the move is constant across the stage and changing according to the body.

(ii) The ring RF – HL – BD was used to contrast with a dimensional "backcloth" of two dancers, in held relationship. Stage orientation was used, with F being stage LF. Both arms impulsively gather to RF, back of the hands leading to nearly touch, weight on the left foot, the move repeated but small; turn to the left in a rounded chord the dominant direction being right arm in LH and trunk tilted to LH, the leg bent behind, the left arm DL; the turn was one complete plus a half to arrive with direction stage BD in front of the dancer. A sliding fall into that direction, right leg sliding, right arm supporting near the hip, and sliding to lie on the right back flank.

(iii) The flat, steep, and flowing inclinations appeared, separated, in a dance, reiterated several times, as the dominant lines from head to foot of three lifts as part of a love duet:

(a) used FD to HL, diving down holding onto his ankle, and he holding her ankles;

(b) used HL to RB, across her partner's shoulders, behind his head;

(c) used RB to FD, held by his arm and supported on his left hip and thigh.

(iv) A chordic position arrived at after a jump: left knee and arm in LF; kneeling, right knee and right arm DR, out-turned both; trunk with head leaning BH.

Example (iii) Five-rings

(a) Logical form

Five-rings (see Fig. 26 on p. 209) are the simplest form of peripheral rings. They are circular and are formed by joining the five places which surround any one planal corner. There are twelve five-rings, and they belong in paris, each pair having one link in common, as follows:

	Link
around FH is	HL – HR – RF – FD – LF – HL
around BH is	HL – HR – RB – BD – LB – HL
around BD is	DL – DR – RB – BH – LB – DL
around FD is	DL – DR – RF – FH – LF – DL
around HL is	LB – LF – FH – HR – BH – LB
around DL is	LB – LF – FD – DR – BD – LB
around HR is	RF – RB – BH – HL – FH – RF
around DR is	RF – RB – BD – DL – FD – RF
around RB is	BH – BD – DR – RF – HR – BH
around LB is	BH – BD – DL – LF – HL – BH
around RF is	FH – FD – DR – RB – HR – FH
around LF is	FH – FD – DL – LB – HL – FH

(b) Body utterance of five-rings.

Five-rings are mostly connected with gesture rather than total body movement. Their performance enriches the vocabulary of gesture, by pointing to the many areas around the body in which gestures of arm and leg can be made. These rings can be performed as either gathering or scattering movements, with one arm leading or both arms together. Some of the deep rings can best be done by the legs, particularly those around DL and DR. Dancing is full of five-rings. They, with the dimensional peripheral moves in the octahedron, form excellent recognition models of sweeping arms and legs.

However they also appear as chords and spatial tension with several parts of the body involved. For example:

(*i*) A travelling sideways repetitive motif using deep second position (DL and DR) as the obvious statement. The arms are LF and RF on the shoulders of two other people who are joined in a circle facing in. The head is circling but comes to FH to synchronise with the second position, causing a chordic statement of the five-ring (the one which is top of the list and in the diagram).

(*ii*) Another door plane five-ring was used consecutively: the arms above the head, lower arms horizontal stating HL–HR, shuffling jump, repeated, symmetric, forwards, rhythmic, knees thrust forward in FD. Every now and then the arms flung out, one after the other RF and LF, only to repeat again the horizontal hold.

3. NUMERICAL RELATIONSHIP OF FORMS WITH A COMMON AXIS

The Primary Scale is the foundation of all other scales and rings, almost. It is a way of linking adjacent locations of the icosahedron so that a curved zigzag path is made up and down an axis; it passes from plane to plane sequentially. One such scale is:

HR — RB — BD — DR — RF — FD — DL
DL — LF — FH — HL — LB — BH — HR

By numbering the locations of the Primary Scale 1 — 12 all other rings and circuits on the same axis can easily be found by numerical formula:

Numerical Relationships of Forms with a Common Axis

Primary Scale	1 2 3 4 5 6 7 8 9 10 11 12
Peri six-ring (evens)	2 4 6 8 10 12
Trans six-ring (odds)	1 3 5 7 9 11

Planes (up in threes)	1 4 7 10
	  2 5 8 11
	    3 6 9 12

Trans three-rings
   (up in fours even)
	2 6 10
	    4 8 12

Peri three-rings
   (up in fours odd)
	1 5 9
	   3 7 11

Trans twelve-rings
   (up in fives)
	1 6 11
	   4 9
	  2 7 12
	    5 10
	   3 8

Mixed seven-rings
   (three odd +
   four even)
	1 3 5 6 8 10 12
	  2 3 5 7 8 10 12
	  2 4 5 7 9 10 12
	  2 4 6 7 9 11 12
	1 2 4 6 8 9 11
	1 3 4 6 8 10 11

It will be seen that transversal six-rings go up in twos on the odd numbers. By referrring to the Primary Scale mentioned earlier, presuming that HR is 1, it will be seen that this transversal six-ring is:

$$HR - BD - RF - DL - FH - LB - HR.$$

Try placing the original Primary onto another axis, by an F/B transposition. Hence:

$$HR - BF - FD - DR - LB - BD - DL$$
$$DL - LB - BH - HL - LF - FH - HR.$$

Finding the peripheral six-ring on this axis; go up in twos, evenly. Hence:

RF – DR – BD – LB – HL – FH – RF.

Finding the *second* mixed seven-ring on this axis:

RF – FD – LB – DL – LB – HL – FH – RF.

Anyone can find forms if they follow these simple syntactic rules.

4. USING THE FORMS

From watching choreographies it is clear that whole forms, especially the longer, more complex ones, are not apparent. This is hardly surprising; no piece consists of logical mathematically-based series alone. One does not hear musical works which continuously go up and down scales, no modern work at any rate. No, fragments are used, sometimes in reverse and in all sorts of body utterance. That the forms are there is not in doubt, but it is easier to look simply for flat, steep, flowing, dimensional and diagonal fragments first, and thereby increase one's vision of what these things look like.

That works of art are organised logically is also not in question. One has only to look at contemporary music and spatially stressed painting to hear and see it quite clearly. So it is with dance. When dance ideas are processed into movements, this logical spatial scheme is one way of doing it, just as schematic use of dynamics is another. Alternatively, improvisation can come first, and the spontaneous utterances can be subjected to syntactic scrutiny and adjusted or developed according to choreutic and dynamic schemes.

Many beautiful and technically demanding sequences and motifs can be made, through which performing skills can be increased. The very mobile transversal movements form a wonderful contrast to the more stable forms of much popular technique, which tends to be octahedrally geared.

Choreutic forms can readily be used towards creative dance making, to provide variety and contrast for technical achievement and to form a reference reservoir for appreciating the logical forms of dance works.

Bibliography

Argyle M. *Psychology of Interpersonal Behaviour.* Penguin 1967

Arnheim R. *Art and Visual Perception.* Faber & Faber 1956

Benesh R. and J. *Introduction to Benesh Movement Notation.* Dance Horizons 1956

Berger R. *The Language of Art.* Thames & Hudson 1963

Birdwhistell R. L. *Kinetics and Context.* Penguin 1970

Bruner J. S. *The Growth of Skill.* Norton, New York 1973

Clarke M and Crisp C. *Ballet, an Illustrated History.* A. C. Black, London 1973

Cohen S. J. *Dance as a Theatre Art.* Harper Row, New York 1974

Cohen S. J. *The Modern Dance, Seven Statements of Belief.* Wesleyan Univ. Press, Connecticut 1965

Connolly K. and Bruner J. S. (eds) *The Early Growth of Competence.* Academic Press, London 1974

Cratty B. J. *Movement Behaviour and Motor Learning.* Lea & Febiger 1973

Critchlow K. *Order in Space.* Thames & Hudson, London 1969

Davis M. *Understanding Body Movement.* Arno Press, New York 1972

De Mille A. *The Book of the Dance.* Hamlyn, London 1963

Ellfeldt L. *Dance, From Magic to Art.* W. C. Brown, Iowa 1976

Ellfeldt L. *A Primer for Choreographers.* National Press Publishing Corp., Palo Alto 1974

Eshkol N. and Wachman A. *Movement Notation.* Weidenfeld & Nicholson 1958

Field D. and Newick J. *The Study of Education and Art.* Routledge & Kegan Paul, London 1973

Gardner H. *The Arts and Human Development.* Inter Science 1973

Geidion-Welcker C. *Contemporary Sculpture.* (3rd edition) Faber 1960

Ghiselin B. (ed) *The Creative Process.* Penguin 1952

Ghyka M. C. *The Geometry of Art and Life.* Dover 1977

Gibson J. J. *The Senses Considered as Perceptual Systems.* Houghton Mifflin, Boston 1966

Hayes E. R. *Dance Composition and Production.* Ronald, New York 1955

H'Doubler M. *Dance, A Creative Art Experience.* Wisconsin Univ. 1957

Hinde R. A. (ed) *Non-Verbal Communication.* Cambridge Univ. Press 1972

Hirst P. H. "Liberal Education and the Nature of Knowledge." in *Education and the Development of Reason.* ed. R. F. Dearden, P. H. Hirst and R. S. Peters Routledge & Kegan Paul, London 1972

Horst L. and Russell C. *Modern Dance Forms.* Dance Horizons, New York 1961

Hospers J. (ed) *Introductory Readings in Aesthetics.* Free Press, New York 1969

Hudson L. *Contrary Imaginations.* Methuen 1966

Humphrey D. *The Art of Making Dances.* Grove, New York 1959

Hutchinson A. *Labanotation.* Theatre Arts Books, New York 1970

Kepes G. *Module Symmetry and Proportion.* Braziller 1966

Koestler A. *The Act of Creation.* Routledge & Kegan Paul, London 1964

Knust A. *A Dictionary of Kinetography Laban (Labanotation).* Macdonald & Evans 1979

Laban R. *Effort.* Macdonald & Evans 1947

Laban R. *Modern Educational Dance.* Macdonald & Evans 1948

Laban R. *Mastery of Movement.* Macdonald & Evans 1960

Laban R. *Choreutics.* Macdonald & Evans 1966

Laban R. *Principles of Dance and Movement Notation.* Macdonald & Evans 1975

Lamb W. *Posture and Gesture*. Duckworth 1957

Lange R *The Nature of Dance*. Macdonald & Evans, Plymouth 1975

Langer S. K. *Feeling and Form*. Routledge & Kegan Paul, London 1953

Lawson J. *Classical Ballet: Its Style and Technique*. Black, London 1960

Le Corbusier *The Modular*. Faber, London 1954

Lyons J. *Theoretical Linguistics*. Cambridge Univ. Press 1968

Nadel H. M and G. N. *The Dance Experience*. Praeger, New York 1970

North M. *Personality Assessment through Movement*. Macdonald & Evans, London 1972

Osborne H. *The Art of Appreciation*. Thames & Hudson 1970

Perry L. "Education in the Arts." in *The Study of Education and Art*. ed. Field D. and Newick J. Routledge & Kegan Paul, London 1973

Piaget J. *The Origin of Intelligence in the Child*. Routledge & Kegan Paul, London 1953

Polanyi M. *Knowing and Being*. Routledge & Kegan Paul, London 1969

Preston-Dunlop V. (ed) *Dancing and Dance Theory*. Laban Centre 1979

Preston-Dunlop V. *Practical Kinetography*. Macdonald & Evans 1969

Preston-Dunlop V. *Readers in Kinetography Laban* (Series B) Macdonald & Evans 1967

Redfern H. B. *Concepts in Modern Educational Dance*. Kimpton, London 1973

Reid L. A. *Meaning in the Arts*. Geo. Allen, London 1969

Rose C–L. *Action Profiling*. Macdonald & Evans, Plymouth 1978

Rogers L. R. *Sculpture*. Oxford Univ. Press 1969

Scheffler I. *Conditions of Knowledge*. Scot Foresman 1965

Schilder P. *The Image and Appearance of the Human Body*. International Univ. Press, New York 1950

Shahn B. *The Shape of Content*. Harvard, Cambridge Mass. 1967

Sherbon E. *On the Count of One*. National Press, Palo Alto 1968

Smith J. *Dance Composition.* Lepus 1976

Sweigard L. E. *Human Movement Practice.* Dodd Mead, New York 1974

Todd M. *The Thinking Body.* Dance Horizons 1968

Torrance E. P. and Myers R. E. *Creative Learning and Teaching* Dodd Mead, New York 1970

Van Praagh P and Brinson P. *The Choreographic Art.* A. C. Black, London 1970

Vernon P. E. (ed) *Creativity.* Penguin 1970

Weyl H. *Symmetry.* Princeton Univ. Press 1953

Whiting H. T. A. *Concepts in Skill Learning.* Lepus, London 1975

Wigman M. *The Language of Dance.* Macdonald & Evans, London 1966

Wilson P. S. *Interest and Discipline in Education.* Routledge & Kegan Paul, London 1971

Winearls J. *Modern Dance, The Jooss-Leeder Method.* Adams & Black, London 1968

Witkin R. *The Intelligence of Feeling.* Heinemann, London 1974

Young M. *Knowledge and Control.* Macmillan, London 1966 (esp. Bourdieu P. "Intellectual Field and Creative Project.")

Index

The general arrangement of the material in this book is shown in the Contents list on pages x–xiii.